Skagit Valley Fare

Skagit Valley Fare

A COOKBOOK
CELEBRATING BEAUTY AND BOUNTY
IN THE PACIFIC NORTHWEST

LAVONE NEWELL

Bon Appétit !

Lavone Newell

ISLAND PUBLISHERS
ANACORTES WASHINGTON
1996

Second printing.

Cover painting by Alfred Currier, Anacortes, WA.

Books may be purchased directly from the publisher by writing:
Island Publishers, Post Office Box 201, Anacortes, WA 98221.

Library of Congress Cataloging-in-Publication Data

Newell, Lavone, 1931-
Skagit Valley Fare: a cookbook celebrating beauty and bounty in the
Pacific Northwest / Lavone Newell.
p. cm.
Includes index.
ISBN 0-9615580-5-9
1. Cookery, American—Pacific Northwest style. 2. Skagit Valley
(Wash.)—Description and travel. I. Title.
TX715.2.P32N48 1996
641.59795—dc20
96-6820
CIP

Table of Contents

For Kiearah, my first great grandchild.

Born with only one hand, she holds in it her world of family and friends.
May those lovely solemn eyes be ever blessed with love and kindness.

Preface

FOR THE PAST TEN YEARS, I have dreamed of writing a book that would integrate my interest in cooking, in the arts, and in the local history of my home region. The Skagit Valley, with its abundant vegetables and fruits, fresh seafood and meat, is indeed a cook's paradise, and I have collected recipes all of my adult life. Sitting around a table with good food, exchanging stories with love and laughter creates an ambiance that warms the heart. It is a most tangible expression of love.

In my earliest memory, I stand as a four-year old on a kitchen chair with one of my mother's aprons covering my entire body as I watched her cook. At that time, I was given the cake batter spoon to lick. When I finished, my chair was placed in front of a dishpan filled with soapy water and I was allowed to wash the dishes. By age twelve, I was the family baker, producing countless loaves of bread, always baking the cakes and cookies.

Art, for me, had its first expression in food decoration. Family-event cake decoration became my forte. Later on, as an older college student, I immersed myself in a smorgasbord of painting, drawing, and writing, with a minor in art history as dessert. Now art is a way of life.

Another driving force in my life is an interest in those who have gone before, the pioneers who left other homes, often other countries, to carve the cultural foundation that makes the Valley what it is today. My rustic home is filled with historic relics. Found wood has been integrated throughout, most with bits of history attached—water-sculpted boards from an ancient dam found floating downriver, logs and chains from parts of log booms found on the beach, wagon wheels and wheelbarrows worn by time and use.

This book is a tribute to the Skagit Valley pioneers, to all those who have worked the land and to all the cooks, past and present, who have spent their lives preparing and preserving food. It is also a celebration of the many artists who have found spiritual inspiration and sustenance in the Valley—the painters, poets and writers, sculptors, crafts people, and musicians who have shared their creativity with the region and beyond. And it is especially a commemoration of my mother, Vera Gough Stone, a woman of modest means throughout her life but always someone of substance.

—LAVONE NEWELL
Fir Island, Washington

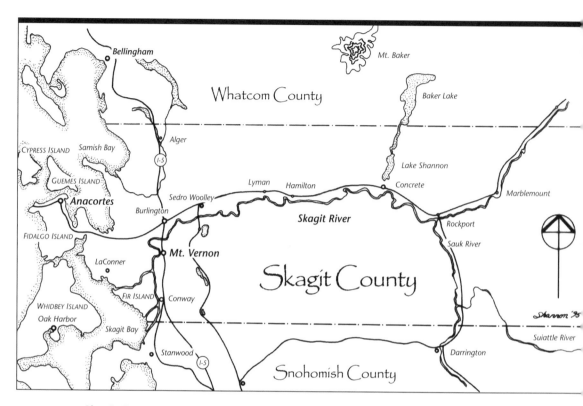

Skagit County comprises only 2.6% of Washington State, but its 1700 square miles of scenic beauty, its abundant fruit and vegetable crops, tulip and daffodil fields, and its attraction to tourists more than make up for its relatively small size. Central to the County's natural abundance is the Skagit River whose green waters rush down from the Cascade Mountains and flow westward across the Skagit Valley to Puget Sound.

Introduction

LAND OF PLENTY

THE SKAGIT VALLEY IN NORTHWESTERN WASHINGTON STATE spills like a great cornucopia from the foothills of the Cascade Mountain Range westward to the waters of Puget Sound. Meandering through these lowlands, the Skagit River and her tributaries continually enrich the Valley's sandy alluvial soil. In the distance, snow-capped Mount Baker stands sentinel above this fertile farmland—some of the richest in the world.

Also known as the Skagit Flats, this area grows a wide variety and volume of crops for national and international markets, producing much of the world's green pea and vegetable seed crops, as well as significant numbers of daffodil and tulip bulbs. Many of these flowering bulbs are exported to Holland where they are then imported back into the United States.

Throughout its gentle marine seasons, the Skagit Flats' colors and textures flow uninterruptedly like living patterns onto the giant canvas of the fields. In March, great swaths of daffodils dazzle the landscape with shades ranging from creamy white to sunny yellow; gradually these early colors are interspersed with the deeper yellows of seed-crop blossoms such as cabbage and rutabaga.

Each April, the valley brightens further as the vast tulip fields blossom, drawing thousands of visitors to The Skagit Valley Tulip Festival to wander among and photograph the brilliant blooms. The giant palette glows with shades of light pink to the deepest purple, and waxy whites contrasting with Christmas reds. Occasionally, a field of mixed tulips appears like some outrageous expanse of confetti fallen from the sky.

Spring is also the time of year when great fields of raspberry and blueberry bushes unfold their tiny creased leaves. When apple, pear, cherry, and plum trees become low clouds of pink and white against the blue skies. Now farm laborers, who earlier worked in the tulips, bend their backs over strawberry fields. The roadside stands that sold flowers a month ago open again, this time selling sweet field-ripened berries the size of small plums.

Summertime in the Valley brings an explosion of rapidly growing plants that provide abundant bounty for local cooks, as well as fruits and vegetables for canneries and frozen food plants. Now juxtaposed fields of white and lavender potato blossoms create breathtaking checkerboards of color among the corn, cucumbers, broccoli, cauliflower, and peas.

Slowly, almost imperceptibly, the colors of summer turn into the oranges and yellows of pumpkin and squash, and the gold of wheat and barley. Pea viners clatter far into the night like dimly lighted locusts to finish harvest in time; trucks heaped high with potatoes and cucumbers rumble off to market. Now the orchards of apples, pears and plums ripen to succulence and cauliflower matures to its purest snowy white.

Another snowy white appears in late autumn as thousands of snow geese, ducks, and swans return from the north to winter under the sulky skies of the Skagit Flats. A program called "Barley for Birds" pays local farmers a stipend to plant winter barley for these visitors whose droppings are later plowed into the soil for rich fertilizer.

Winter colors in the Skagit Valley are the browns and tans of unplanted fields, the subdued greens of seed crops and the white wings of birds that swoop in and out to forage slowly through puddled fields. For a few short months, the land lies dark and quiet. Then the cycle begins again when local residents exclaim, "Look! The daffodils are coming up." And, sure enough, there they are—heralding yet another spring.

The Skagit Valley ends at the shores of Puget Sound, but Skagit County extends to several islands of the San Juan Archipelago: Fidalgo and Samish Islands connected to the Flats by bridge; Guemes served by a ferry; and Cypress by boat or air. These shores and islands inspire poets and painters with their shifting moods and colors, and their waters provide seafood for the gourmet cook. Though not as plentiful as in the recent past, salmon and crab, mussels, oysters, clams and scallops, as well as various kinds of cod fish, are still available on the fresh market.

It is no wonder that the Native Americans who lived here were peaceful and contented with their way of life. They enjoyed a mild marine climate, quiet coves and beaches, expanses of forest where mushrooms and other edible plants could be gathered, plentiful wild game, and seafood more abundant than we can ever imagine today.

This book is a celebration of the Skagit Valley. Along with recipes from our best cooks and restaurants, there are stories about pioneers and present-day people, as well as art and poetry in praise of the magic Skagit.

—THELMA J. PALMER

Skagit History Notes

ELEVEN NATIVE INDIAN TRIBES were the first documented inhabitants of the Skagit Valley. They were hunters and gatherers who found mushroom, roots, herbs, and berries in the wooded areas where deer, bear, and smaller game were also plentiful. In the Skagit River and coastal waters, salmon, cod, and sea mammals were abundant, and the beaches provided mussels, oysters, and clams.

The first European-American settlers arrived in the Skagit Valley in the mid-1800s. The new residents were accepted by the native Indians who often helped them to harvest timber and farm crops. The Indians bartered fish and seafood with the settlers for tradegoods and money and impressed them with their skills on the river in their flat-nosed canoes—the "first Skagit Taxis."

Early-day settlers tended to cluster with others from their home country or area. They formed at least half a dozen ethnic communities, starting in the last half of the 1800s. The Swedes concentrated in the LaConner area and at Hoogdal (north of Sedro Woolley); the Norwegians settled around Conway and Edison; the Finn settlement was near Lake McMurray.

Mining had its day in the Valley's Cascade Mountains between 1880 and the early 1900s. With the prospectors came road builders and merchants. Hydroelectric development of the Skagit River and its tributaries started in the 1920s. Today there are four dams: Ross, Diablo, Gorge, and Baker.

Around the turn of the century, with the coming of the railroad to the Upper Valley, Italians and Greeks arrived to work the limestone quarries that were the lifeline of the cement industry at Concrete. At the same time, the North Carolina hill people from the Smoky Mountains, most often referred to as "Tarheels," formed the basis for Skagit's logging industry. The Tarheels settled in Lyman, Hamilton, and the Rockport-Marblemount area, while Croatian and Scandinavian fishermen were drawn to the fertile waters around the Anacortes area. All of these groups are still a part of the Valley's heartbeat.

Skagit Valley's attraction for artists began in the 1930s. "The Mystic Painters of the North West," profiled by *Life* in 1953, drew their inspiration from the Valley's natural beauty and luminous atmosphere. Morris Graves, one of the most revered artists in the United States, lived in LaConner and, later, on Fidalgo Island in a clifftop cabin called "The Rock." Guy Anderson still lives in LaConner, Richard Gilkey on Fir Island. The other internationally renowned artists of that group, Mark Tobey and Kenneth Callahan of Seattle, often visited the Skagit Valley.

Many musicians, poets, and writers have found sustenance for their creativity in the area. The 1950s brought Jack Kerouac and Gary Snyder here, working for the United States Forest Service as fire lookouts atop the Cascade Mountains of the Upper Valley. One could not find a better place for solitude and introspection. Best-selling author Tom Robbins has just finished his sixth novel while living in the LaConner area. In the late Betty Bowen's Fishtown community on the banks of the North Fork of the Skagit, poets, painters, and writers found a haven. They lived with the mud and night creatures, blessed by the soft gray light of morning mists and the spectacular sunsets of summer. It was a sad day for the art community when its buildings were razed and Fishtown was finished.

The rich farmland of the lower Valley has, over the years, drawn seasonal workers from Mexico and today supports a year-round Hispanic citizenry. In many ways, the

Skagit Valley today is a kaleidoscope of change. There is still an agricultural base, but logging has slowed to a trickle, while development of industry, malls, and housing is on the rise. Too, Skagit Valley is now a tourist Mecca. It has become known world-wide for its tulip fields and recreational diversity.

Skagit County has many fine restaurants, inns, and bed and breakfasts where visitors can sample inspired presentations of local fare. It is my hope that this book will contain an honest representation of Skagit cooking from its beginnings to the present. It includes family recipes handed down from generation to generation; recipes handed from friend to friend; recipes left behind by visitors. All have been sampled by willing tasters. Now it's your turn to enjoy a taste of past and present!

—LAVONE NEWELL

Acknowledgments

I WOULD LIKE TO EXPRESS MY GRATITUDE to publishers Thelma Palmer and Delphine Haley for their advice and assistance along the way and especially for asking me if I was interested in writing a cookbook. To Jim Poth of Easy Going Outings for giving them my name and background in cooking. To artist Al Currier whose cover painting captures the essence of the Valley in spring.

Heartfelt thanks go to my computer coaches Ann Childs, Rick Carlson, and Stephen Thornton. They pulled me from the brink of disaster numerous times over the last eighteen months. I would not advise others to follow my technique of becoming computer literate while writing a first book! A big thank you also goes to granddaughter, Chantelle Hilsinger, for entering recipes in the computer during crush times and to Doug Walker for transferring my work from the borrowed Mac computer I started with to the IBM compatible that I now own.

I want to thank the following artists for allowing me to use photographs of their art work: Guy Anderson, Al Currier, Richard Gilkey, Morris Graves, Clayton James, Anne Martin McCool, Philip McCracken, and Maggie Wilder.

Thank you to the following photographers: Cathy Pearson Stevens for the author's photograph and photographs of paintings by Anne Martin McCool and Maggie Wilder. Chris Eden for the photograph of Guy Anderson's painting. And Dick Garvey for the cover photograph of Al Currier's painting, as well as photographs of paintings by Clayton James.

I would also like to recognize and thank the following poets: James Bertolino, Clifford Burke, Jean Hallingstad, Peter Heffelfinger, Paul Hansen, Thelma Palmer, Bill Slater, Robert Sund, and Glen Turner.

It would take many pages to list all of the friends, relatives, and Skagitonians who generously shared bits of family history along with their favorite recipes. Some, like Mac and Linda McGregor and Bekky Love, turned over entire recipe boxes and collections handed down by mothers and grandmothers. Others shared individual antique cookbooks that had belonged to their ancestors. I cherish the feeling of trust and belief in this book created by that generosity. My only regret is that I could not use all of the contributions and stories that have been collected.

I wish to thank the following Skagit Valley businesses for sharing some of their favorite recipes:

Calico Cupboard Cafe & Bakery
720 South First Street, LaConner, WA, 360/466-4451

Calico Cupboard Old Town Cafe & Bakery
901 Commercial Avenue, Anacortes, WA, 360/293-7315

El Gitano Mexican Restaurant
624 E Fairhaven, Burlington, WA, 360/755-9010

White Swan Guest House
1388 Moore Road, Fir Island, WA, 360/445-6805

Hope Island Inn
1686 Chilberg Road, LaConner, WA, 360/466-3221

Dona Flora Herbs and Flowers
Box 77, LaConner, WA, 360/466-3964

Farmhouse Inn
1376 LaConner-Whitney Road, LaConner, WA, 360/466-4411

Lighthouse Inn
512 South First, LaConner, WA, 360/466-3147

Wild Iris Bed and Breakfast
121 Maple Avenue, LaConner, WA, 360/466-1400

Skagit Valley Food Co-op
202 South First, Mount Vernon, WA, 360/336-9777

The Riverhouse
50465 First Street, Rockport, WA, 360/853-8557

Alice Bay Bed and Breakfast
982 Scott Road, Bow, WA, 360/766-6396

Blau Oyster Company
919A Blue Heron Road, Bow, WA, 360/766-6171

Captain Whidbey Inn
2072 West Captain Whidbey Inn Road, Coupeville, WA, 360/678-4097

*Amanda picked the Skagit Valley up by its damp green heels and shook
its whole stash of goodies out onto our table. She shook out a silver salmon,
big as a baby, baked with a sour cream glaze. There were fresh oysters,
both steamed and raw. Late broccoli in a hot sauce with overt sadistic
tendencies. Corn on the cob. Burdock tubers. Cattail roots. Biscuits baked
from cattail pollens. Four varieties of wild fungus: chanterelles, meadow
mushrooms, lepiota and king boletus. Cow parsnip (the stems were peeled
and eaten raw like celery). Roasted lady-fern stalks. Creamed onions. Lichen
soup. Pine nuts. Wild honey. Starfish eggs. Pumpkin pudding. Apples. Pears.
And so forth and so on, all of the food having been gathered by the Zillers
free of charge, as is still possible in Skagit County despite the toxic cement
encroachment of industrial horrors.*

—TOM ROBBINS
Another Roadside Attraction

Winter Still Life, Morris Graves

APPETIZERS

SUNFLOWER

The package said "Sunflower Seeds."
Instead, there grew in my garden
a tall woman with pale round face
and a scalloped bonnet.
This morning she hung her head
in the rain, and, later
when I went to shake the drops,
she bent down and kissed me,
blessed me
with all the seeds of her countenance.

—THELMA PALMER

Caviar Pie

From Guemes Island an impressive appetizer by Anne McCracken, former high school English teacher, owner of Piping Rabbit Press, and wife of sculptor Philip McCracken, whose Exploding Potato *is found on page 145. This recipe can be made a day ahead.*

SERVES 10 TO 12.

6 hard-boiled eggs

3 tablespoons mayonnaise

1 1/2 cups finely chopped Walla Walla or sweet white onion

8 ounces softened cream cheese

2/3 cup sour cream

1 4-ounce jar caviar (Romanoff lumpfish is fine)

Fresh parsley for garnish

CHOP EGGS fine and combine with mayonnaise in small bowl.

BUTTER BOTTOM AND SIDES of a springform pan and spread egg mixture in even layer over the bottom.

SPRINKLE CHOPPED ONIONS over egg mixture.

BLEND softened cream cheese with sour cream and spread over onion layer with wet spatula.

CHILL OVERNIGHT or longer.

JUST BEFORE SERVING, top with caviar. Decorate with parsley.

REMOVE RIM of springform pan. Serve pie with crackers or melba toast.

Oven Barbecued Chicken Wings

Skagit Valley artist Anne Martin McCool, whose painting appears on page 205, makes this quick and easy dish.

SERVES 6 OR MORE.

3 pounds of chicken wings, cut off tips

1/2 teaspoon cayenne pepper

2 tablespoons oil

1 cup honey

1/2 cup soy sauce

1/2 clove garlic, chopped

2 tablespoons catsup

PREHEAT oven to 350°.

IN A LARGE BOWL, mix oil with cayenne pepper. Toss wings in mixture until coated.

ARRANGE WINGS in a single layer in shallow baking dish.

COMBINE remaining ingredients and drizzle over wings.

BAKE for 1 hour or until coating has caramelized and wings are very brown.

Asparagus Guacamole

Sue Karahalios, former Washington State legislator, makes this delightful fat-free substitute for avocado guacamole. If you double the recipe for a large gathering, be sure to blend only one-half at a time to prevent overloading your blender motor.

MAKES APPROXIMATELY 3 CUPS, OR 24 2-TABLESPOON SERVINGS.

1 1/2 pounds fresh asparagus or 21 ounces of frozen or canned

1/2 teaspoon garlic powder

4 teaspoons lime or lemon juice

4 tablespoons chopped canned green chilis

2 tablespoons chopped onion

1 teaspoon crushed red peppers

4 teaspoons tomato paste

1/4 teaspoon salt

1/2 teaspoon ground cumin

1/4 teaspoon ground ginger

STEAM ASPARAGUS until tender, 10 to 12 minutes.

DRAIN WELL. Pat dry with paper towels and place in blender.

ADD remaining ingredients and blend until smooth.

SERVE with crackers or chips.

Smoked Oyster Dip

Jo Ann Welling, one of the Valley's great cooks, serves this dip with Hot Cheese Wafers.

MAKES 2 CUPS.

1/2 cup black olives, chopped

1 3-ounce can of smoked oysters, drained and chopped

1 cup low fat sour cream

1/4 cup parsley, chopped

3 green onions, chopped

2 tablespoons high quality mayonnaise

1 tablespoon lemon juice

1/2 teaspoon salt

1/4 teaspoon Tabasco sauce

MIX ALL OF THE INGREDIENTS together. Serve with crackers or as a vegetable dip.

Hot Cheese Wafers

MAKES 92 WAFERS.

1 cup margarine

1/2 pound sharp cheddar cheese, grated

2 cups all-purpose flour

1/2 teaspoon garlic salt

1/2 teaspoon cayenne pepper

2 cups crispy rice cereal

PREHEAT OVEN to 375°.

IN A MEDIUM BOWL, cream margarine and cheese.

MIX IN FLOUR, garlic salt, and cayenne pepper.

STIR IN crispie rice cereal.

FORM into 3/4-inch balls, place on ungreased cookie sheet, and flatten into 2-inch diameter rounds.

BAKE for 10 minutes or until edges are lightly browned. Wafers may be frozen unbaked. Store baked wafers in air-tight container.

Gruyère Crackers

Most good cooks have one thing in common: when you ask them for a recipe they usually say, "But I don't measure; I just cook." French-born chef Marie-Paule Braule is a good example of this phenomenon. When teaching cooking classes at the White Swan Guest House on Fir Island, she encouraged her students to experiment liberally and not to measure precisely. Following are four of the appetizer recipes she shared.

SERVES 24.

4 1/2 ounces Gruyère cheese, grated

1 cup flour

1/2 cup cold butter, cut in small pieces

Dash cayenne pepper

3 1/2 tablespoons sour cream

PREHEAT OVEN to 350°.

IN FOOD PROCESSOR or with pastry cutter, work cheese, flour, butter, and cayenne until mixture resembles coarse meal.

ADD SOUR CREAM and pulse in processor or work with hands until mixture forms dough.

ROLL DOUGH into log shape and wrap in plastic film. Chill for one hour.

SLICE ROLL into 1/4-inch rounds.

BAKE on buttered cookie sheet 17 to 20 minutes, or until lightly golden.

Marie-Paule's Salmon Spread

MAKES 1 1/2 CUPS.

8 ounces cream cheese, room temperature

1/4 cup whipping cream

1 green onion, chopped

1 teaspoon lemon juice

Dash Tabasco sauce

4 ounces smoked salmon

2 tablespoons salmon caviar

BLEND CREAM CHEESE and whipping cream until smooth.

STIR IN remaining ingredients gently, leaving salmon in small chunks. Serve with your favorite crackers.

Marie-Paule's Indonesian Crab Canapés

SERVES 24.

3 tablespoons lemon juice

1 garlic clove, minced

1/4 cup roasted unsalted peanuts, coarsely chopped

1 tablespoon vegetable oil

1/4 teaspoon cayenne pepper

1/2 cup mayonnaise

1/4 pound lump crab meat

3 tablespoons green onion, chopped

Salt and pepper to taste

French bread, sliced and toasted, with crusts removed

Chopped parsley for garnish

PREHEAT oven to 450°.

BLEND LEMON JUICE, garlic, peanuts, oil, and cayenne pepper.

COMBINE with mayonnaise, crab, and onion. Add salt and pepper.

CUT FRENCH BREAD into small squares and spoon dollop of topping on each.

BAKE for 10 minutes.

SPRINKLE with chopped parsley and serve.

Mushrooms Véronique

SERVES 18.

18 mushrooms

18 green seedless grapes

5 ounces Boursin cheese

1/4 cup melted butter

1 cup fresh-grated parmesan cheese

Pepper to taste

PREHEAT oven to 400°.

STEM MUSHROOMS.

WIPE with paper towel to clean.

PLACE 1 grape in each mushroom cap.

PLACE 1/2 teaspoon of Boursin cheese on top, enclosing grape completely.

ROLL IN melted butter and then in parmesan cheese.

REFRIGERATE at least 20 minutes or up to 1 day.

BAKE for 15 minutes.

SPRINKLE with remaining parmesan and serve.

Vegetarian Stuffed Mushrooms

This recipe comes from the kitchen of Peter Goldfarb, proprietor of the White Swan Guest House, a gracious Victorian home on Fir Island. See Peter's Potato Leek Soup, Ginger Peachy Pecan Muffins, *and* Skagit Berry Muffins *in other sections of this book.*

SERVES 10.

20 large mushrooms

2 tablespoons butter

1 small onion, chopped

2 cloves garlic, minced

1 tablespoon olive oil

1/2 cup golden raisins

1/3 cup chopped walnuts

1/2 cup bread crumbs

1 egg, whipped lightly with a fork

2 tablespoons fresh chopped parsley

Dash of Worcestershire sauce

2 tablespoons catsup

Salt and pepper to taste

PREHEAT oven to 350°.

REMOVE AND CHOP stems from mushroom caps.

SAUTÉ onion and garlic in butter and olive oil until browned.

ADD chopped mushroom stems and cook just until wilted.

RUB mushroom caps with olive oil and place round side down in large baking pan.

STIR hot onion mixture in bowl with raisins, walnuts, bread crumbs, raw egg, and parsley.

ADD Worcestershire sauce, catsup, and seasonings. Stir until combined.

SPOON mixture into mushroom caps and bake for 20 minutes.

Brie In Bread

This old favorite has graced many local buffet tables.

SERVES 24.

1 round or oval loaf day-old French bread

1/3 cup butter, softened

2 cloves garlic, finely minced

1 to 1 1/2 pounds of Brie cheese, cut into 1-inch cubes

PREHEAT oven to 350°.

HOLLOW OUT bread carefully, leaving 1/2-inch shell. Save center for cubing.

AROUND TOP rim of shell make decorative cuts. Cut the center bread into 1 1/2-inch cubes.

BLEND butter with garlic. Brush mixture over inside of bread shell and on cubes.

PLACE cheese inside bread shell, with or without the rind.

PLACE cheese-filled shell and cubes on cookie sheet.

BAKE for 10 minutes.

REMOVE bread cubes from cookie sheet. Return shell to oven and bake until cheese melts. This should take about another 10 minutes.

SERVE hot cheese-filled bread on a large platter, surrounded with cubes for dipping.

Panae "Beaver Bread"

This tantalizing appetizer with an Italian twist is from the "Beaver Club," a group of long-time friends who meet occasionally to exchange barbs and recipes.

MAKES ABOUT 30 1/2-INCH SLICES.

1 loaf of frozen bread dough, thawed

1/2 green pepper, chopped

1/2 red sweet pepper, chopped

1/2 orange sweet pepper, chopped

1 medium onion, chopped

1 to 2 cloves garlic, minced

2 tablespoons olive oil

1/2 teaspoon dried oregano

1/2 teaspoon dried sweet basil or Italian herbs

1/4 pound thin-sliced ham

1/4 pound thin-sliced Swiss cheese or mozzarella

1 tablespoon or more, black olives, sliced

1 6-ounce jar marinated artichoke hearts, drained and chopped

1 egg white for glazing

PREHEAT oven to 350°.

ROLL OUT thawed dough to the size of a cookie sheet.

SAUTÉ peppers, onion, and garlic in oil and season with herbs.

PLACE ham slices on long side of rolled-out dough, covering up to 2/3 of it, leaving about a 2-inch border.

PLACE cheese slices on ham. Cover with sautéed vegetables, olives, and artichokes.

ROLL UP dough lengthwise, jelly-roll fashion, and brush top with slightly beaten egg white. Place on oiled cookie sheet.

BAKE for 10 minutes or until lightly browned and cheese is melted through.

ALLOW TO SET for a few minutes before cutting into 1/2-inch slices.

Layered Appetizer Torte

This three-layer torte is another of Jo Ann Welling's specialties.

SERVES 25 TO 30.

24 ounces cream cheese
1/4 cup butter

BLEND well together and divide into 3 portions.

LAYER 1:

1/3 of cream cheese mixture
4 to 6 ounces ham, precooked sausage or salami, finely minced
1 tablespoon white onion, minced
Dash of Tabasco sauce

COMBINE minced meat, onion, and Tabasco. Spread mixture in bottom of glass baking dish lined with cheesecloth. Smooth well and chill.

LAYER 2:

1/3 cream cheese mixture *above*
1/4 pound cheddar cheese, grated
2 tablespoons milk.

COMBINE cream cheese mixture, cheddar, and milk until blended. Spread over Layer 1 and chill.

LAYER 3:

1/3 cream cheese mixture *above*
4 green onions

WASH, dry, and slice green onions, including tops. Purée in food processor. Drop remaining cream cheese mixture into onion while processor is running. Spread over Layer 2.

CHILL overnight. Garnish with parsley and serve with your favorite crackers.

NOTE: Recipe can be halved for a smaller gathering.

Chilled Asparagus With Sesame Vinaigrette

Valley visitor Betsy Schiff has served this refreshing appetizer at our family dinner gatherings and received many compliments.

SERVES APPROXIMATELY 8.

2 pounds trimmed fresh asparagus spears

2 tablespoons plus 2 teaspoons sesame oil

1 tablespoon plus 1 teaspoon rice vinegar

1 tablespoon plus 1 teaspoon soy sauce or tamari

1 teaspoon sugar

1/4 cup sesame seeds, toasted

Salt and pepper to taste

COOK ASPARAGUS till crisp and tender. Rinse with cold water and drain well.

PAT DRY with paper towels and arrange on platter. Refrigerate until ready to serve.

COMBINE sesame oil, rice vinegar, soy sauce, and sugar in small bowl and stir until sugar is dissolved.

SEASON to taste with salt and pepper.

JUST BEFORE SERVING, spoon vinaigrette over chilled asparagus and sprinkle with toasted sesame seeds.

Pickled Herring

Pickled herring is a staple of the Swedish smorgasbord tradition brought to the Valley in the 1800s. The late Sig Berglund developed this recipe and shared it in a Vasa Lodge cookbook. The Vasa Lodge was formed in Skagit County in 1920 and was one way for Swedes to get together and maintain their homeland traditions. Pickled Herring is part of any Swedish gathering and is almost always on the Christmas buffets.

SERVES 12 TO 14.

3 firm salted herring (*available in markets at Christmas*)

1 medium onion, sliced in thin rings

PLACE HERRING in cold water to cover and soak overnight.

PREPARE pickling brine *(below)* and refrigerate overnight.

NEXT MORNING, skin herring and bone it. Cut down the back of the fish to remove backbone and pull the skin from the tail of fish upwards.

WASH fish and pat dry with paper towels to help keep brine clear.

BE SURE all bones are removed and cut fish into bite-sized pieces.

IN GLASS BOWL, layer fish and onions. Pour pickling brine over all and refrigerate for at least 24 hours before serving.

BRINE:

1 cup apple cider vinegar

1 cup water

1 cup sugar

1 teaspoon whole allspice

1 teaspoon whole cloves

COMBINE liquids, sugar, and spices in saucepan and bring to gentle boil. Simmer 10 to 15 minutes.

COOL and refrigerate overnight.

Penn Cove Mussels Poached In Pale Ale

Phyllis McKee is an inventive gourmet cook who often invites friends over for an evening of dining. And the dining does take all evening—seven courses, each with its own wine or champagne. This appetizer makes superb use of local fare.

MAKES 4 TO 6 SERVINGS.

3 pounds Whidbey Island Penn Cove mussels or mussels of choice

15 cloves garlic

12 sprigs fresh thyme, each about 3 inches

1 bottle Bridge Port Blue Heron Pale Ale

1/2 cup whipping cream

IN A COVERED SAUCEPAN, place cleaned mussels along with remaining ingredients.

BRING TO A BOIL. Turn heat off. Leave covered for approximately 10 minutes.

SPOON MUSSELS and broth into soup plates and serve as a first course with a dry Washington white wine, such as St. Michelle Semillon, '92.

Captain Whidbey Ginger-Steamed Mussels

The Captain Whidbey Inn was established in 1907 on Penn Cove Bay. Many Skagitonians travel there to enjoy the Inn's specialty, Penn Cove mussels, prepared in numerous ways. Ginger-Steamed Mussels is a favorite. Chefs Roger Porter and Joan Strouse developed this recipe.

SERVES 4 TO 6.

3 tablespoons ginger, chopped

1 1/2 cups green onions, chopped, both green and white parts

4 cloves garlic, minced

1 tablespoon coarse black pepper

6 chili peppers, small, hot, seeds removed, finely diced

3 tablespoons sesame oil

3/4 cup rice wine vinegar

1/3 cup soy sauce

1 1/2 cups sake

4 dozen fresh mussels, scrubbed and debearded

IN A LARGE MIXING BOWL, combine all ingredients except mussels.

PLACE above ingredients in large saucepan. Add rinsed and dried mussels.

COVER PAN tightly and cook over medium heat until mussels open—about five to seven minutes.

DISCARD any that do not open.

REMOVE FROM HEAT and swirl to coat mussels with sauce.

SERVE in warmed bowls with sauce ladled over mussels.

NOTE: Recipe yields approximately 30 ounces of sauce. It will keep in the refrigerator for 2 weeks.

LAST SUNSET OF THE YEAR 1975 : FISHTOWN

Crystal sunset on the Skagit, a stain level, stark and clear,
Burns rose red and ochre, Ika Island's hunched up spine
Leaps trembling like a doe as molten high slack waters shine,
Naked-alder-dangling catkins adorn solstice and new year.

Fishtown lamp and silence, solitary cure and cheer
For hermit, fool or clown ensnared in passion's searing night,
Will soothe slowly, will ship wholly into sky-arched bays of sight
Past stark headlands, within vision, unsailed waters near.

LINES ON BEING POOR

An aging apprentice in poverty's school,
Kin say I'm a cowardly weak-hearted fool,
Up cold in the morning, bed hungry at night,
Spare lessons recited in clear steady light.

For the stove, this dry alder, a friend brought it by;
Walking boardwalks at midnight, I see the bright sky.
A song flares within me; stars kindle the chill.
What people call sorrow is half of God's will.

—PAUL HANSEN

Dreadful Ox Tail Soup

John Hall, an entrepreneur with wide-ranging business interests, came to Avon, Skagit County, in 1890. His wife was an excellent cook who prepared this nurturing soup. Their daughter Frances recalls the recipe as follows:

SERVES 4.

"This recipe always began with, 'Run over to the slaughter house and ask Uncle Joe for an ox tail.'

"When my sister or I returned with the dreadful thing, our mother would wash it well, cut it up at the joints, then dredge the pieces lightly with flour and gently brown them in butter.

"Then she added 1 1/2 quarts of cold water, which she brought to a boil and simmered until the meat fell from the bones.

"At this point she cooled the ox tail in the 'cooler' overnight.

"Next day she skimmed off the fat and added 3 or 4 carrots cut into chunks, chopped 1 rutabaga, 2 potatoes, 1 large onion, 1 leek, and 3 stalks of celery and added 1 teaspoon of salt.

"She cooked the soup until the carrots were tender, then corrected the seasoning, adding more salt, some pepper, and dill weed to taste.

"The 'Dreadful Ox Tail' became our richest, favorite soup."

Mom's Navy Bean Soup

I have a warm childhood memory of trudging homeward from the Faber Ferry landing where the school bus dropped us off. My pace quickened dramatically when the aroma of simmering navy bean soup and fresh-baked bread reached me. As an afterschool snack, we children were allowed to have a cup of the soup broth and a thick slice of warm bread for sopping. I don't think I have ever eaten anything that tasted better.

SERVES 6 TO 8.

2 to 3 cups navy beans, rinsed and soaked for a couple of hours

1 to 1 1/2 pounds of smoked ham hock

Pinch of soda

1/2 to 1 teaspoon salt or to taste

1/2 teaspoon fresh-ground pepper

1 large onion, minced

1 cup celery with leaves, chopped fine

1 to 2 teaspoons dried herbs (*Mom used a mixture of thyme, sage, basil, and rosemary*)

Water to fill 6 to 8-quart stock pot

PLACE the soaked beans in stock pot with ham hocks.

ADD WATER until 3 inches below top of the pot. Bring to a boil; add soda, salt, and pepper. Lower heat and simmer.

SAUTÉ the prepared vegetables with herbs in butter or oil before adding to soup.

KEEP WATER LEVEL above beans and meat as they simmer, stirring occasionally with wooden spoon.

WHEN HAM is falling off hocks, 1 1/2 to 2 hours, remove hocks from soup and cool enough to remove bones, fat, and skin.

BREAK HAM into bite-sized pieces and return to soup pot.

ADJUST seasonings if necessary. Sometimes I add garlic salt and dried onion flakes if soup needs a bit more flavor.

Don't forget to bake the bread!

Split Pea Soup

From valley visitor Betsy Schiff, this soup is suitable for Sunday night supper in front of the fire or a simple luncheon any day.

SERVES 8.

3 to 4 cups dry green split peas

2 quarts water, or more if needed

1 bay leaf

Salt to taste

1 ham hock

2 tablespoons oil

1 cup onion, minced

3 cloves garlic, crushed

1 cup celery, minced

1 small peeled potato, thinly sliced

2 cups carrots, sliced

1/4 cup dry red wine

1/4 teaspoon dry mustard

1 teaspoon dried thyme

Few drops sesame oil

3 tablespoons vinegar

1 cup tomato, chopped

1/4 cup parsley, chopped

COMBINE split peas, water, bay leaf, and ham hock in a large soup pot and simmer for 3 hours.

REMOVE bay leaf and ham hock.

SHRED ham off bone and return ham to soup.

SAUTÉ onion, garlic, celery, potato, and carrots in oil until tender. Add to soup.

ADD wine, dry mustard, thyme, and sesame oil to simmering soup.

JUST BEFORE SERVING, add vinegar, tomato, and parsley. Ladle into soup bowls and serve.

Greek Chicken Soup With Lemon

A soup from an old church cookbook. The well-spattered page indicates it has been a favorite.

SERVES 8 TO 10.

1 whole stewing chicken or fryer

1 large onion, chopped

1 cup celery including leaves, chopped

3 quarts water

1 cup raw rice

2 eggs

Juice of 1 lemon

Salt to taste

Fresh-ground pepper to taste

PLACE rinsed chicken in large stockpot and cover with cold water.

BRING TO A BOIL. Skim off foam.

ADD finely chopped onion and celery and simmer, covered, over low heat for 2 1/2 hours or until chicken falls from bones.

REMOVE from heat and strain. Return the broth to sauce pan.

RINSE rice and add to broth and simmer until rice is cooked.

WHILE RICE IS COOKING, remove chicken from bones and shred or cube.

WHEN RICE IS TENDER, return chicken pieces to simmering pot.

BEAT eggs in mixing bowl until thick and lemon-colored.

ADD lemon juice and seasonings to taste.

CONTINUE BEATING and slowly add 2 cups hot chicken stock. Constant beating will prevent curdling.

RETURN THIS MIXTURE to pan and continue to beat until well mixed. Heat to just below boiling point and serve immediately.

Lentil & Brown Rice Soup

From my files, a comforting soup for a rainy day.

SERVES 6 TO 8.

5 cups chicken broth
1 1/2 cups lentils, rinsed
1 cup brown rice
1 32-ounce can tomato juice
3 carrots, sliced 1/4-inch thick
1 large onion, chopped
1 stalk celery, chopped
3 cloves garlic, peeled and sliced
1/2 teaspoon dried basil
1/2 teaspoon dried oregano
1/4 teaspoon dried thyme
1 bay leaf
2 tablespoons vinegar
1/2 cup fresh parsley, chopped

COMBINE all ingredients, except fresh parsley and vinegar. Reserve those to add when soup is fully cooked.

SIMMER lentil-rice mixture for at least 1 hour or until cooked to right consistency.

WHEN DONE, stir in vinegar and place in soup bowls.

SPRINKLE with parsley and serve.

Black Bean Soup With Rum

Rum adds extra warmth to this hearty cold-weather soup.

SERVES 6 TO 8.

2 cups onion, chopped

1 cup celery, chopped

1/4 cup parsley, chopped

1/4 teaspoon dried thyme

1 bay leaf

1 large ham hock

2 cups black beans, soaked overnight in
    cold water

6 cups beef broth

1/3 cup rum

4 cups water

Juice of 1 lemon

GARNISH:

Parsley sprigs

Grated lemon rind

Hard-boiled egg, chopped

SIMMER all ingredients in non-reactive stockpot for 3 hours.

STIR soup occasionally. If it becomes too thick, thin with water.

JUST BEFORE SERVING, remove bay leaf and ham bone. Shred meat off with a fork and return it to soup pot.

SERVE soup garnished with bits of parsley, lemon rind, and hard-boiled egg.

Port & Pig Soup

This is a favorite of this book's cover artist Al Currier and his wife Regina.

SERVES 6.

1 1/2 pounds Italian sausage, cut into 1/2-inch slices

1 tablespoon olive oil

2 large onions, chopped

2 cloves garlic, minced

28 ounces canned Italian-style tomatoes with liquid

42 ounces canned beef broth

1 1/2 cups port wine of choice

1 teaspoon basil leaves, crumbled

2 medium zucchini, cut into 1/4-inch slices

1 medium green pepper, seeded and chopped

3 tablespoons parsley, chopped

2 cups bow macaroni

5 ounces parmesan cheese, grated

IN LARGE KETTLE, sauté sausage slices until lightly browned.

DRAIN and discard most of fat.

ADD onions and garlic and sauté until onions are limp.

STIR in tomatoes, breaking them into small pieces with a fork.

ADD broth, wine, and basil and simmer one hour.

REMOVE FROM HEAT, cool, and refrigerate. Skim off fat when chilled.

RETURN TO SOUP POT and stir in zucchini, green pepper, and parsley. Add cooked and drained bow macaroni.

COVER and simmer for about 15 minutes or until all vegetables are cooked but still crisp.

SERVE with grated cheese.

Mushroom Stroganoff Soup

This wholesome soup was created by Linda Freed, who serves country-style breakfasts and lunches, heart-smart and vegetarian entrees, whole grain breads, tantalizing pastries, and desserts in her two Skagit Valley restaurants, the Calico Cupboard in LaConner and the Calico Cupboard Old Town Cafe and Bakery in downtown Anacortes. Linda cooks everything from scratch and it tastes like it! (You will find her recipe for Quiche Santa Fe *on page 70.)*

SERVES 6 TO 8.

2 medium potatoes, thinly sliced

4 cups chicken broth

1 medium onion, diced (about 1 cup)

1/2 teaspoon ground bay leaves

12 ounces sliced mushrooms

2 tablespoons butter

2 1/2 tablespoons soy sauce

1/2 teaspoon paprika

1/4 teaspoon dried thyme

1/2 teaspoon dried marjoram

1 teaspoon dried sweet basil

1/4 cup parsley, chopped

1 teaspoon celery seed

1 teaspoon garlic, minced

6 ounces cream cheese

3 ounces cheddar cheese, grated

1/4 cup sour cream

3/4 cup milk

3/4 cup frozen peas

5 ounces whole-wheat egg noodles

COMBINE potatoes, chicken broth, 1/4-cup of the onion, and bay leaf in saucepan. Simmer until potatoes are tender.

SAUTÉ remaining onion and mushrooms in butter.

ADD remaining ingredients to soup and simmer until noodles are tender, about 10 to 12 minutes.

Fresh Sorrel Soup

The following Latvian recipe was given to me by my friend Ausma. At the end of World War II, she and her mother fled Latvia before the Russian army moved in to claim the country. For several years they lived in refugee camps. In one, they were reunited with Ausma's father, who had been in the Latvian army fighting against the German invasion. As I write this, Ausma, her Texan husband and their three adult children are making a pilgrimage to her Latvian birth-place fifty years after her flight.

SERVES 3 TO 4.

1 smoked ham butt

1 large whole onion

2 to 3 bay leaves

1 dozen peppercorns tied in cheesecloth

2 to 3 cups fresh sorrel leaves, chopped*

1 cup spinach leaves, chopped

1/2 cup barley or quick oats

1 cup sour cream

2 to 3 hard-boiled eggs, chopped, for garnish

*Available in season at specialty produce markets.

IN A LARGE SOUP POT, cover ham with cold water, bring to a boil and skim off foam.

SIMMER slowly for one hour or more.

ADD onion, bay leaves, and peppercorns.

WASH, chop, and blanch sorrel and spinach. Add to soup along with barley or oats.

COOK until grains are tender but not mushy, 10 to 30 minutes.

REMOVE onion, spices, and ham bone. Remove skin and fat from ham. Shred meat and return to soup.

STIR in sour cream until blended. Serve with chopped hard-boiled egg garnish.

NOTE: The soup can also be made with all spinach, adding vinegar to taste to replicate the tartness of sorrel.

Stinging Nettle Soup

Every year I look forward to nettle soup made from the first spring growth in March and early April. I grew up with wild greens as staples in our food supply—young dandelions, lamb's quarter, miner's lettuce. Nettles, a good source of Vitamin C and minerals, should be picked in unsprayed areas only. Take just the top 4 inches and always wear gloves.

SERVE 12.

1 gallon (16 cups) young nettle tops, lightly pressed down with gloved hands

1 quart (4 cups) French sorrel greens, washed

2 medium onions, finely chopped

2 cloves garlic, minced

4 medium-sized potatoes, peeled and cut into small chunks

2 tablespoons olive oil

1 teaspoon salt or to taste

4 cups chicken broth

1/2 teaspoon pepper, freshly ground

1/2 teaspoon nutmeg, freshly grated

1 to 2 tablespoons butter

1 cup half-and-half or milk

WITH GLOVED HANDS, cut any heavy stems from nettle tops, then wash tops well.

IN LARGE SAUCEPAN, fry onions and garlic for 4 minutes in olive oil .

ADD chicken broth and bring to boiling point.

ADD potatoes and simmer for 5 minutes before adding nettles and sorrel.

SIMMER until potatoes are tender and nettle greens are cooked.

TRANSFER the hot mixture to a food processor or blender and liquefy at high speed. You may need to do it in more than one batch. A blender makes a smoother soup.

RETURN SOUP to saucepan to keep hot. Add seasonings and butter.

JUST BEFORE SERVING, stir in the half-and-half. Do not boil. Serve with crusty bread.

Leek-Potato Soup

This wholesome soup can be served hot or cold.

SERVES 4 TO 6.

4 leeks, cleaned and chopped, white part only

1 medium onion, chopped

2 tablespoons butter

4 medium white potatoes, peeled and cubed

2 14 1/2-ounce cans chicken broth

1 1/2 cups milk or half-and-half

Salt and pepper to taste

Chopped chives for garnish

MELT butter in skillet and sauté leeks and onion over low heat until transparent.

ADD potatoes and chicken broth. Cover and simmer for 15 minutes or until potatoes are tender.

PUT THROUGH food mill or food processor.

RETURN to saucepan and add milk. Season to taste with salt and pepper.

WHEN HEATED, but not boiling, serve in bowls with sprinkling of chives or chill and serve cold.

Roasted Red Pepper And Coconut Milk Soup Striped With Petite Pea Purée

If you want to impress, this is the recipe. Phyllis McKee and I originated this red-white-and-green soup to impress the publishers. It drew rave reviews and does so every time it is served.

SERVES 5 TO 6.

RED PEPPER PURÉE:

1 15-ounce jar of roasted red bell peppers

1/4 cup chicken broth*

1 14-ounce can coconut milk**

1 large sweet white onion, coarsely chopped

1 tablespoon extra-virgin olive oil

6 cloves garlic

*A 14 1/2-ounce can serves for both recipes.

**Available in Asian food section of supermarkets.

IN A SKILLET, sauté onions and garlic in oil until transparent.

ADD chicken broth and simmer, covered, for approximately 10 minutes.

IN A BLENDER, blend onion-garlic mixture, peppers, and coconut milk until smooth, approximately 3 minutes.

TRANSFER purée to saucepan. Heat just before serving.

PETITE PEA PURÉE:

1 10-ounce package frozen petite peas, thawed

1 1/2 cups chicken broth

6 sprigs fresh spearmint or other mint

IN A BLENDER, combine peas, chicken broth, and mint until smooth.

TRANSFER purée to saucepan. Heat to below boiling point to retain *fresh* green pea color.

SERVING INSTRUCTIONS: With the aid of a companion or with a ladle in each hand, begin pouring a ladleful of each soup purée from opposite sides into serving bowls. Soups will meet, but not blend. Garnish each bowl with a sprig of mint and a splash of crème fraiche or sour cream.

Chilled Eggplant Parsley Soup

The following recipe was given to me by my good friend April Kulp who weekends in a cabin on Pull and Be Damned Road, Swinomish Reservation. It is a great soup to serve on a hot July day.

SERVES 4.

1 eggplant, 1 pound
2 teaspoons salt
1 onion, minced
1 tablespoon olive oil
2 cloves garlic, minced
1 teaspoon curry powder
4 1/2 cups chicken broth
1/4 cup parsley, minced
Juice of one fresh lemon

CHOP eggplant and toss with salt.

DRAIN for 20 minutes in colander.

RINSE with cold water and drain again.

SAUTÉ onion in oil in heavy covered saucepan, over low heat, approximately 3 minutes, stirring occasionally.

ADD GARLIC and cook for 1 minute.

ADD CURRY and cook for 1 minute.

ADD BROTH and bring to a boil.

ADD EGGPLANT and simmer for 40 minutes.

PURÉE the above mixture in a blender or food processor by batches.

SEASON with salt and pepper to taste.

COOL and chill for at least 2 hours.

STIR in lemon and sprinkle with chopped parsley and serve.

Norwegian Fruit Soup

Early Valley pioneers John Christian Vike, born in Norway, and his wife, Karn Nokelby Vike, born in America of Norwegian parents, arrived at the early settlement of Fir on the lower Skagit Delta in the 1800s. Their granddaughter, Pauline Hunter Heath, remembers her grandmother's Norwegian cooking, particularly the following fruit soup. The soup's flavor changed as different fruits ripened or when canned fruits were used. Pauline recalled that her mother Jennie preferred canned native wild blackberries (dewberries, often found on logged-over areas in July) as the main ingredient for this refreshing soup. It is equally good served hot or cold.

SERVES 4 TO 6.

1 quart canned or fresh Italian prunes or fruit of choice

1/2 cup raisins

1/2 cup dried currants

1 cup apple, peeled and diced

3 cups water

3/4 cup sugar

1/2 cup pearl tapioca

1/2 lemon, with peel, cut in paper-thin slices.

1/2 orange, with peel, cut in paper-thin slices.

1 cinnamon stick

COMBINE prunes, raisins, currants, apple, and water in a large saucepan.

BRING TO A BOIL over medium heat. Simmer for 45 minutes, stirring to prevent sticking.

ADD sugar, tapioca, lemon slices, orange slices, and cinnamon stick.

CONTINUE TO COOK, stirring often, for another half hour. Remove cinnamon stick.

SERVE hot or chill. Can be served as a dessert or as part of a meal. For a thinner soup, stir in fruit juice of your choice—orange, apricot, or berry—during last few minutes of cooking.

NOTE: Can be served over hot cereal for breakfast with a handful of fresh raspberries, sliced strawberries, or sliced bananas sprinkled over the top.

Skagit Bouillabaisse

Julie Rousseau, author of the popular Alice Bay Cookbook, *created this Skagit version of a classic seafood dish. She lives on a beautiful Skagit Valley waterway and has only to walk down the path to the bay to harvest oysters, clams, and crab.*

SERVES 16.

2 tablespoons olive oil

3 medium onions, chopped

4 stalks celery, chopped

1 green pepper, diced

2 carrots, sliced

3 cloves garlic, minced

2 cups dry white wine

2 cups clam nectar or fish stock

2 28-ounce cans of whole tomatoes, cut up

1 quart tomato juice or Snappy Tom

Dash of hot pepper sauce

1 teaspoon of saffron

1/2 teaspoon fennel seed, crushed

2 bay leaves

4 pounds whitefish fillets, cut into 1 or 2 inch pieces

2 pounds bay scallops

24 steamer clams, steamed and drained (reserve the nectar)

24 blue mussels, steamed and drained

2 pounds shrimp, shelled and deveined

1/4 cup fresh parsley, minced

Freshly ground pepper to taste

HEAT OIL in large skillet or soup pot. Add onions, celery, green pepper, carrots, and garlic. Sauté until transparent, about 3 minutes.

ADD WINE, clam nectar or fish stock, tomatoes with their juice, tomato juice, hot pepper sauce, saffron, fennel seed, and bay leaves. Simmer for 5 minutes.

ADD FISH pieces and scallops. Simmer for 5 to 7 minutes.

STIR IN clams, mussels, shrimp, and parsley. Simmer for 3 to 5 minutes, until shrimp are tender and clams and mussels are heated through.

SPOON into large bowls and serve piping hot. With sourdough French bread and a green salad this bouillabaisse is a complete meal.

Lavone's Italian Fish Soup

This is my version of traditional Italian fish soup. It is a meal in itself when served with fresh-baked sourdough French bread.

SERVES 6 TO 8.

1/2 pound fresh sweet or hot Italian sausage

3 tablespoons olive oil

1 medium onion, diced

3/4 cup celery including leaves, chopped

1 small red sweet pepper, chopped

1 small yellow sweet pepper, chopped

3 14 1/2-ounce cans Italian-style chopped tomatoes with basil

4 medium potatoes, diced

1 teaspoon salt

Fresh-ground pepper to taste

4 cups fish stock or clam nectar

1 pound firm white fish, such as cod or halibut, cut into chunks

1/2 pound fresh scallops

1/2 pound of fresh cooked and peeled medium sized shrimp

1/2 cup dry white wine

1/4 cup fresh parsley, chopped

1 tablespoon lemon juice or to taste

1 teaspoon lemon zest

3 dashes Tabasco sauce

IN LARGE SOUP POT, sauté Italian sausage until lightly browned in olive oil. Add onion, celery, and peppers and continue to sauté until vegetables are limp.

ADD TOMATOES, potatoes, salt, pepper, and fish stock to sautéed vegetables and bring to a simmer.

COOK for about 10 minutes and then add fish and scallops. Simmer for 5-7 minutes.

ADD SHRIMP, wine, half of the parsley, lemon juice, lemon zest, and Tabasco. Bring back to a simmer and serve immediately.

SERVE in large soup plates with remaining chopped parsley sprinkled over the top.

GARDENS

Gardens are more than
hooded flowers, tempting fruits
and living trees.
They are the birds
that sing and fly in them,
the wing-eyed butterflies,
the golden bees.
They include the sky
with sun and moon and stars,
the rain and snow
they are the earth
with captured light from heaven
where plants and people grow.
A garden is a universe
that whispers soft and vernal,
"As it is above, so it is below."
Waking, blooming, sleeping,
waking up again,
gardens are eternal:
they teach us all we need to know.

—THELMA PALMER

Fresh Skagit Greens With Pinenuts And Raspberry Vinaigrette Aioli

Weekend farmers' markets throughout the Skagit Valley are a good source for the mixed fresh greens featured in this sweet-tart salad.

SERVES 5 TO 6.

Use any or all of the following washed and crisped greens (about two handfuls per person).

Oriental mustard

Baby lettuce

Young sorrel leaves

Rhubarb Swiss chard

Arugula

Escarole

Green chard

Spinach

Parsley

Generous handful pinenuts

PLACE greens in salad bowl.

TOSS greens with Raspberry Vinaigrette Aioli below.

RASPBERRY VINAIGRETTE AIOLI:

2 cloves fresh garlic

2 tablespoons raspberry vinegar

1 egg

1/4 teaspoon lemon herb seasoning

1/4 teaspoon lemon pepper

1 cup extra-virgin olive oil

PLACE all ingredients, except oil, into blender and pulse until combined.

WITH BLENDER ON HIGH, pour in oil in a steady stream. You will notice a significant sound change in the blender as the mayonnaise thickens.

TOSS greens with vinaigrette dressing. Place on over-sized salad plates and garnish with a generous portion of pinenuts.

Summer Salad

Conway Hill resident Jean Keith, a friend from high school days in Concrete, gave me this recipe.

SERVES 6.

1 head romaine lettuce, torn

1 head red leaf lettuce, torn

1 bunch spinach, torn

2 cups canned mandarin orange sections, drained

1/2 pound bacon, cooked, drained, and crumbled

1/2 medium red onion, thinly sliced and separated into rings

1/2 to 1 cup feta cheese or fresh-grated parmesan

COMBINE salad ingredients in large bowl. Toss with dressing *(below)*.

DRESSING:

1/4 cup sugar

1 teaspoon grated onion or 1/2 teaspoon onion powder

1 teaspoon dry mustard

1 teaspoon salt

1/3 cup vinegar

1 cup vegetable oil

1 teaspoon poppy seeds

1 teaspoon sesame seeds

COMBINE all ingredients in covered jar and shake well.

Spinach & Strawberry Salad

Jana Svendsen of Mt. Vernon and Betty Crippen of Clear Lake are my sources for a colorful salad reflecting the Valley's summer harvest.

SERVES 4 TO 6.

2 bunches washed and crisped spinach,
    torn
1 pint fresh strawberries, sliced

DRESSING:

1/3 cup sugar

2 tablespoons sesame seeds

1 1/2 teaspoons minced dry onion

1/4 teaspoon Worcestershire sauce

1/4 teaspoon paprika

1/4 cup cider vinegar

1/2 cup salad oil

COMBINE all dressing ingredients and toss with spinach and strawberries.

NOTE: For a lighter dressing, cut the sugar in half and substitute fresh orange juice for one-half of the oil.

Spinach Salad Flambé

From Father Paul Dalton, who visits on the Swinomish Reservation, an elegant holiday salad. Be very careful while igniting the brandy.

SERVES 4 TO 6.

Flame-proof salad bowl

Tossing utensils

2 bunches spinach

3 lemons

10 slices bacon

4 eggs

1/4 cup sunflower seeds

1 tablespoon vinegar

2 tablespoons brown sugar

1/2 cup brandy

CLEAN spinach. Tear into bite-sized pieces, roll in towel, and chill.

HARD-BOIL the eggs. Cool, peel, slice and place on the edge of a plate.

CHOP the bacon slices and fry. Remove bacon and save the grease.

To the bacon drippings, add the vinegar and brown sugar. Can add more sugar and vinegar to taste.

PUT SPINACH in a large bowl and squeeze 2 of the lemons over the spinach while tossing. Add 1/4 cup sunflower seeds. Save remaining lemon for garnish.

REHEAT bacon-grease dressing and pour over spinach. Toss.

REHEAT bacon in a second skillet and add brandy. Light brandy and pour over salad.

SERVE immediately on a plate with lemon wedges and egg slices arranged on the edge of the salad.

Caesar Salad

Andreas Enderlein, a frequent visitor to the Skagit Valley, is known for this recipe. Whenever he asks what he can bring to dinner, the instant response is "Caesar salad."

SERVES 4.

3 to 4 garlic cloves, smashed and chopped

1 green onion, chopped

1 tablespoon strong mustard

1 tablespoon fresh parsley, chopped

Salt and pepper to taste

3 tablespoons wine vinegar

3/4 cup olive oil

Few drops lemon juice

1 large romaine lettuce, washed and dried

1 package garlic-flavored croutons

6 anchovy filets, drained

1/2 cup fresh-grated parmesan cheese

PLACE garlic, shallot, mustard, and parsley in bowl and add seasonings.

POUR in vinegar and mix well with a whisk.

ADD oil in steady stream, whisking constantly.

CORRECT SEASONING if needed and add a few drops of lemon juice.

TEAR lettuce leaves into large pieces and place in salad bowl. Add croutons and toss briefly.

ADD anchovy filets, pour in vinaigrette, and toss until combined.

SPRINKLE salad with parmesan cheese and toss lightly. Serve immediately.

Feta Cheese Salad
With Green Beans & Walnuts

Marilyn Carlson, longtime friend, gave me the following recipe. It is a favorite.

SERVES 4.

1 1/2 pounds fresh green beans

3/4 cup olive oil

1/2 cup chopped fresh mint

1/4 cup white wine vinegar

3/4 teaspoon salt

1/4 teaspoon pepper

1 clove garlic, minced

1 cup toasted walnuts, chopped

1 cup red onions, diced

1 cup feta cheese, crumbled

STEAM beans until crisp tender.

DRAIN and plunge into ice water to stop cooking.

DRAIN and pat dry with paper towels.

COMBINE oil, mint, vinegar, salt, pepper, and garlic in blender until smooth.

PLACE beans in serving bowl and pour dressing over them.

ADD onions, walnuts, and feta cheese.

TOSS well.

Marilyn's Mixed Greens With Hazelnut Dressing

Another of Marilyn Carlson's salads featuring Skagit Valley's varied farm produce.

SERVES 6 TO 8.

Crisp washed and dried fresh greens, such as baby lettuces, mustard greens, spinach, arugula, or any of your favorites

1 Sliced ripe pear

Roasted hazelnuts for garnish, about a handful

FIRST prepare the dressing *(below)*.

FILL a salad bowl with greens.

POUR prepared dressing over greens and toss lightly.

GARNISH with pear slices and roasted hazelnuts and serve.

DRESSING

1/4 cup cider vinegar

2 teaspoons honey

1 teaspoon grainy mustard

1 teaspoon garlic, minced

1/2 teaspoon shallot, minced

3/4 cup olive oil

1/4 cup hazelnut oil (found in gourmet kitchen shops)

1 teaspoon chopped parsley

Salt and pepper to taste

COMBINE all ingredients in a food processor or blender and blend until smooth.

Four Bean Salad

From long-time Valley resident Dorcelée Coslor comes an old favorite made new with a flavorful dressing.

SERVES 6 TO 8.

2 one-pound cans green beans
1 one-pound can red kidney beans
1 one-pound can yellow wax beans
1 15 1/2-ounce can garbanzo beans

DRAIN beans and turn out into large bowl. Add chopped and sliced onions, garlic, olives, and green pepper.

OPTIONAL ADDITIONS:
2 tablespoons white or purple onion, chopped
Minced garlic to taste
2 or 3 green onions, sliced
Green and/or black olives to taste
1/3 cup green pepper, chopped

DRESSING:
1/2 cup sugar
1 teaspoon salt
1/2 teaspoon dry mustard
1/2 cup canola oil
1/2 cup olive oil
1/2 cup wine vinegar
1/2 teaspoon dried basil
2 tablespoons fresh parsley, chopped
2 or 3 stems of French pickled tarragon (available from gourmet kitchen stores)

BLEND dressing ingredients by beating together or shake well in a jar with a lid.

POUR dressing over bean mixture and marinate overnight.

BEFORE SERVING, stir salad gently and drain marinade.

PLACE individual servings on bed of ruffled red lettuce or other fresh greens. Or serve in a salad bowl.

NOTE: You can substitute fresh tarragon if unable to find pickled tarragon.

Artichoke-Tomato-Feta Salad

This is Mary-Clayton Enderlein's favorite salad for potlucks. It only takes 10 minutes to prepare and is always one of the first to disappear.

SERVES 8 TO 10.

4 8 1/2-ounce cans water-packed artichoke hearts, drained and quartered

8 to 10 Roma tomatoes, sliced

1/2 medium red onion, sliced into thin rings

2 to 4 ounces of feta cheese, crumbled

MIX ingredients in salad bowl.

DRESSING:

1/2 cup light olive oil

2 tablespoons balsamic vinegar

2 to 3 tablespoons fresh basil, chopped

1 tablespoon fresh tarragon, chopped

1 to 2 cloves garlic, minced

Fresh-ground pepper to taste

PREPARE dressing. The longer it sits, the tastier it becomes, but it can be used right away.

POUR dressing over salad. Toss and serve.

Herring Salad

The late Elsa Nelson was well known in the Valley's Scandinavian community for her herring salad, another smorgasbord staple.

SERVES 6 TO 8.

1 salt herring
1 1/2 cups boiled potatoes, diced
1 1/2 cups pickled beets, diced
1/2 cup apple, diced
1/4 cup onion, chopped
1/3 cup sweet or dill pickle, chopped
1 cup celery, chopped
White pepper to taste
4 tablespoons cider vinegar
2 tablespoons sugar
2 tablespoons water

GARNISH:
Parsley sprigs
1 to 2 hard cooked eggs, sliced
Pimento strips (optional)

DRESSING:
1/2 cup canola oil
1/2 teaspoon dry mustard
1 tablespoon sugar
4 tablespoons vinegar
1/2 teaspoon salt
2 raw egg yolks (optional)

SOAK the salted herring in cold water overnight.

NEXT MORNING drain and skin the herring. Remove all bones; wash, and pat dry. Cut into bite-sized pieces.

BLEND sugar, water, and vinegar in mixing bowl. Add salad ingredients and stir.

ARRANGE salad mixture on a platter and pour over dressing below. Garnish with parsley sprigs, egg slices, and pimento strips.

BLEND together well before using.

Chinese Fish Salad

Big Lake area resident Shannon Good, is a fourth-generation Skagitonian. Her Chinese Fish *and* Indonesian Rice *salads are a study in different tastes, textures, and color.*

SERVES 5 TO 6.

1 1/2 pounds fresh, firm fish (halibut, salmon, or cod)

Juice and zest of 2 limes

1/2 cup toasted pinenuts

2 tablespoons black sesame seeds, chopped

1/2 bunch coriander, chopped

6 green onions, julienne

6 tablespoons pickled ginger, julienne

2 to 3 tablespoons pickled jalapenos, chopped

2 packages of ramen noodles, crushed and toasted

SLICE and bone fish and marinate in lime juice for 4 hours.

ADD remaining ingredients, except crushed noodles, and toss with dressing below.

DRESSING:

1/2 to 1 teaspoon of dry mustard

1/2 teaspoon cinnamon

1 tablespoon sugar

3 tablespoons tamari

3 teaspoons sesame oil

2 tablespoons peanut oil, heated

COMBINE dressing ingredients in a small bowl. Just before serving, toss with toasted noodles.

Indonesian Rice Salad

SERVES 4 TO 6.

2 cups cooked brown rice*
1/2 cup raisins
1/2 cup toasted cashews
1 small can water chestnuts, drained
1 small green pepper, chopped
1 small sweet red pepper, chopped
3 to 4 green onions, chopped
1/4 cup sesame seeds
1 cup fresh bean sprouts
A handful of fresh snow peas
1 or 2 stalks celery, chopped
1 8-ounce package firm tofu, cubed (optional)
1/4 cup toasted coconut

Adding a teaspoon of tumeric to rice water will give a golden color to the salad.

COMBINE the above ingredients.

PREPARE dressing *(below)*.

DRESSING:
1/2 cup orange juice
3/4 cup safflower oil
2 tablespoons sesame oil
1 tablespoon hot chili oil
3 tablespoons Tamari or soy sauce
2 tablespoons sherry
Juice of 1 lemon and grated rind of 1 lemon
5 cloves of garlic, minced
1 tablespoon chopped or grated fresh ginger

COMBINE ingredients and blend well.

ADD dressing to rice mixture and mix well.

SERVE on individual dishes or in salad bowl.

Sesame Chicken Salad

Hope Island Inn has hosted notables such as John Wayne, Bing Crosby, and Duncan Hines. Built in 1939 on prime waterfront at SneeOosh, four miles west of LaConner's Rainbow Bridge, it is an ideal spot to enjoy sunsets, serenity, and delicious food. Diners can also browse through and buy the inn's many antique books and art pieces.

SERVES 4.

MARINADE:
1/2 bottle Teriyaki Glaze
1/2 cup light cream
1/4 cup cooking sherry
Dash white pepper

IN A SMALL BOWL, whisk together marinade ingredients.

4 skinless, boneless chicken breasts, marinated for 12 hours before cooking
1 small head romaine lettuce
1 banana
1 kiwi, sliced
1 tangerine, peeled and sectioned
1 to 1 1/2 cup strawberries, halved
Or a selection of seasonal fruit

PLACE chicken breasts in flat dish and pour marinade over them, coating all sides. Refrigerate covered for at least 12 hours, turning chicken periodically.

DRAIN and reserve marinade. Grill chicken over an open flame or under a broiler until cooked through.

WHILE CHICKEN GRILLS, boil the reserved marinade in small saucepan until reduced to half.

GARNISH:
Sesame seeds
Sliced roasted almonds

SECTION each breast and arrange over a bed of romaine scattered with assorted fruit slices.

DRIBBLE the marinade reduction over the completed salad. Garnish with sesame seeds and sliced roasted almonds.

Grandma's Cole Slaw

Roz Spray of Bayview shares a family recipe passed down by her grandmother.

SERVES 4.

1/2 head cabbage, shredded
1 or 2 apples, diced

DRESSING:

1 tablespoon butter
1 tablespoon flour
2 tablespoons sugar
1 egg, beaten
2 tablespoons cider vinegar
3 tablespoons heavy cream

IN A SAUCEPAN, over low heat, melt butter and blend in sugar and flour.

ADD egg and vinegar. Cook over low heat until thick.

REMOVE from heat and beat in cream. Cool.

MIX with cabbage and apples and serve.

Johann's Sunomono Cucumber Salad

A Japanese recipe given to me, an American, by a German! The language of food is truly international. This dish is a good accompaniment for baked salmon.

SERVES 4.

2 long cucumbers
1/3 cup rice vinegar
4 teaspoons sugar
1 teaspoon salt
1 tablespoon fresh-grated ginger root

SLICE cucumbers as thinly as possible on a slicer-grater.

COMBINE the rest of the ingredients in a bowl.

ADD the sliced cucumbers and marinate for at least an hour.

Mom's Molded Cranberry Salad

I can't remember a Thanksgiving or Christmas dinner that didn't include molded salad made with ground fresh cranberries. Even though my mother is no longer living, the tradition carries on. As Christmas Eve draws near, one of my children will inevitably ask, "You are making Grandma Stone's salad, aren't you?"

SERVES 6.

1 3-ounce package raspberry jello

1 cup boiling water

1 tablespoon lemon juice

3/4 cup crushed pineapple with juice

1 cup raw cranberries, ground

1 orange, ground, rind and all

1/2 cup celery, chopped fine

1/4 cup walnuts, chopped

1/2 cup sugar

IN A MIXING BOWL, dissolve jello in boiling water.

ADD lemon juice and pineapple; stir until well mixed.

ADD cranberries, orange, celery, nuts, and sugar to the hot gelatin mixture and stir together until sugar is dissolved.

POUR in mold or flat dish and set in refrigerator to become firm.

NOTE: For my large holiday family, I double the recipe and use either a 9x13 inch flat baking pan or a large mold.

7-Up Salad

Norma Trueman of Lyman takes this salad to family gatherings and everyone loves it.

SERVES 12.

1 6-ounce package of lemon jello

2 cups hot water

2 cups 7-Up

2 cups canned crushed pineapple with juice

2 large bananas, sliced

1 cup small marshmallows

DISSOLVE jello in hot water and cool.

ADD 7-Up and let the mixture stand until it starts to thicken, about 30 minutes.

DRAIN pineapple, reserve juice.

ADD pineapple, bananas, and marshmallows to jello. Pour mixture into a 9x13 glass baking dish. Refrigerate to jell while you make the topping.

TOPPING:

1 cup reserved pineapple juice

1/2 cup sugar

2 rounded tablespoons flour

1 egg, beaten

2 tablespoons unsalted butter

1 cup frozen dairy whip

1 cup cheddar cheese, grated

MIX flour and sugar and combine with pineapple juice in saucepan.

STIR in beaten egg and cook on medium heat until thickened, 5 to 10 minutes.

REMOVE from heat and stir in butter.

WHEN COMPLETELY COOLED, fold in dairy whip.

SPREAD topping evenly over salad. Sprinkle grated cheddar over top.

River Landscape, Richard Gilkey

ENTRÉES

HERON LIGHT

In a flooded tideflat peafield
plowed for the winter
muddy sworls
a fingerprint on glass
abandoned harvester
blower neck crookd and poised
like heron in chipped red
paint and rust
a figure, made with pleasure,
across the high bridge Swinomish.

Coming into the valley through that notch
cut out of Padilla Heights you can see
the light growing up from foothills
clear to the rough Cascades. Where does it
come from? No matter what the sky's like,
the valley, like a dreamscape, lights
itself. Big crusty iron heron fits right in.

Like a figure made with pleasure
by the swamp between the lanes
the real heron
seen both going and coming back
quite still
a heron in the mind.

Heron heading for the trees
ignores the western view of Texaco & Shell.

How the heron perseveres.

Below, the plowed field slopes away
toward Samish Bay, placid at slack water.

—CLIFFORD BURKE

Grandma Stone's Chicken & Noodles

When I was a child, Sunday dinner after church was either chicken and noodles or chicken and dumplings. Saturday's ritual was to choose the extra rooster or pick out the hen that didn't lay eggs. The poor creature was then beheaded or its neck was wrung. Sunday morning, before church, the chicken was put on to boil. Dough for noodles was mixed and rolled out on a floured board. When thin enough, the dough was sprinkled with flour and rolled up like cinnamon rolls, cut into 1/4-inch thick slices, shaken out and spread to dry on a floured surface while we attended church.

SERVES 6 TO 8.

1 stewing chicken or whole fryer

Water to cover

1 teaspoon salt

Fresh-ground pepper to taste

1 tablespoon dried onion flakes or 1 onion, minced

1 tablespoon fresh thyme, minced or 1/2 teaspoon dried

1 tablespoon fresh sage, minced or 1/2 teaspoon dried

1 teaspoon fresh rosemary or pinch of dry

1/2 teaspoon garlic salt or 2 garlic cloves, minced

PLACE cleaned (and skinned, if you prefer) chicken in large stock pot. Cover with water and bring to a boil. Skim off any foam that appears.

ADD remaining ingredients and simmer until meat is falling off bones.

REMOVE chicken from broth with a slotted spoon and set aside to cool enough to remove the meat from the bones and skin. You can do this step one day ahead of time. If you chill the broth, you can remove as much of the fat as you wish before adding the noodles and the flaked chicken meat. The fat does add to the flavor.

ADD noodles *(recipe follows)* or dumplings.

NOODLES:

3 eggs, beaten until thick and fluffy

1 1/2 teaspoons salt

6 tablespoons cream or milk

3 cups flour

COMBINE eggs, salt, and cream or milk.

PLACE flour in mixing bowl. Make a well in center of flour and add egg mixture. Stir until stiff dough.

TURN OUT on a floured board and knead briefly, then roll out very thin. Let stand 20 minutes. Sprinkle with flour and roll up like cinnamon rolls.

SLICE into 1/8 to 1/4-inch slices. Shake out on floured surface and spread to dry on a tea towel. For crisper noodles, dry for a couple of hours or overnight.

NOTE: If in a hurry, roll the dough out very thin and cut into rectangle to fit microwave. Cook on high for 1 minute. Remove, lay on cutting board, and cut into noodles with sharp knife.

DROP into boiling chicken soup and cook for 10 minutes or until tender.

Quiche Santa Fe

A delightful entrée from the Calico Cupboard in LaConner.

SERVES 6.

1 unbaked 10-inch pie crust

1/2 onion, finely chopped

1/4 cup melted butter

7 eggs

2 tablespoons flour

1 teaspoon salt

1 cup salsa

3/4 cup canned green chilies, chopped

Dash cayenne pepper

7/8 cup half-and-half

7/8 cup whipping cream

1/4 cup cheddar cheese, grated

3/4 cup Swiss cheese, grated

3/4 cup black olives, sliced

3/4 cup frozen corn kernels, thawed and drained

1 tomato, sliced

Additional cheese for topping

PREHEAT oven to 375°.

SAUTÉ onion in melted butter.

MIX eggs, flour, salt, salsa, chilies, pepper, half-and-half, and whipping cream thoroughly.

LAYER cheese, onion, olives, and corn in pastry shell.

POUR egg mixture on top.

ARRANGE sliced tomato over top and sprinkle with additional cheese.

BAKE for 45 minutes or until puffy and lightly browned.

Poulet D'artichoke

Quick and easy—a scrumptious combination of flavors.

SERVES 6 TO 8.

2 9-ounce packages frozen non-marinated artichoke hearts, halved

2 to 3 cups cooked, cubed chicken breast

2 10 3/4-ounce cans cream of chicken soup

1 cup mayonnaise

1 teaspoon lemon juice

1/2 teaspoon curry powder

1 cup cheddar cheese, grated

1 1/4 cups soft 1 1/2-inch bread cubes

2 tablespoons melted butter

PREHEAT oven to 350°.

COMBINE artichoke hearts and chicken in large flat casserole.

COMBINE soup, mayonnaise, lemon juice, and curry powder and pour over chicken. Cover with cheese and top with bread cubes, pushing them down slightly into the casserole ingredients.

POUR melted butter over bread. Bake for 25 minutes.

Chicken Poseidon

Crab-stuffed Chicken Poseidon is a gourmet dish from Hope Island Inn. Owners Grant Lucas and Dave Lowrance present each delectable item on their menu with tongue-in-cheek descriptions. For this item, the menu says: "Our Samurai chef hand selects only the finest Kobe chickens, which visitors to the Orient will recognize as the fabled Japanese fowl housed in the gilded cages of the great Shogunate—lovingly massaged and hand fed with succulent truffles three times daily."

SERVES 4.

4 skinless, boneless chicken breasts

1/2 cup fresh Dungeness crab meat

8 ounces lite cream cheese

1/2 cup fresh spinach, chopped

1/2 small sweet red pepper, chopped

1 tablespoon black olives, sliced

1 tablespoon red onion, chopped

PREHEAT oven to 375°.

BUTTERFLY chicken breast or pound between two pieces of waxed paper until about 1/4-inch thick.

COMBINE remaining ingredients in mixing bowl.

PLACE 1/4 of crab-cream cheese mixture on each flattened chicken breast. Fold chicken around it, place in oiled baking dish, and bake 45 minutes to 1 hour until chicken is browned and tender. Alternatively, slice the stuffed chicken in 1/2-inch slices before baking.

WHILE CHICKEN BAKES, make the following sauce to pour steaming hot over the chicken just before serving.

APRICOT-ORANGE SAUCE:

1/4 cup apricot nectar

1/4 cup fresh-squeezed orange juice

1/4 cup heavy cream

1/4 teaspoon white pepper

WHISK ingredients in a small saucepan and heat to a boil. Boil until cream is reduced by half.

ARRANGE baked chicken on serving plate and pour fruit sauce over it.

Citrus Cilantro Chicken

A frequent visitor to the Valley, Karen Roosma, introduced me to this low-fat, high-flavor dish.

SERVES 6.

6 Chicken breasts, boned and skinned

MARINADE:
1/2 cup fresh lemon juice
1/2 cup fresh lime juice
1/2 cup fresh orange juice
1/4 cup dry white wine
1/4 cup olive oil
4 cloves garlic, minced
1 bunch cilantro, chopped
1/2 teaspoon fresh-ground pepper
5 bay leaves

COMBINE and let sit for 1/2 hour so flavors blend.

PREHEAT oven to 350°.

PLACE chicken breasts in marinade, turn to coat, and refrigerate for 2 hours.

DRAIN and reserve marinade. Lay chicken in shallow baking dish. Bake 45 minutes to one hour, basting with marinade at least once to keep chicken juicy. (Or broil chicken, if you prefer.)

SERVE with steamed rice and Rhubarb-Mango Chutney *(page 140)*, a green salad, and fresh-baked bread.

River House Chicken Breast

A recipe from the old River House at Rockport.

SERVES 2.

1 split chicken breast

1 1/2 cups Chablis wine

2 tablespoons teriyaki sauce

1 tablespoon ground oregano

2 tablespoons granulated onion

1/4 teaspoon garlic powder

1 heaping teaspoon dried basil leaves

1/2 cup mushrooms, sliced

Chopped parsley and paprika for garnish

BROWN chicken breast, skin side down, in hot oiled skillet.

COVER AND COOK approximately 20 minutes or until tender.

BONE chicken breasts and place skin side down in 1-quart saucepan with Chablis.

ADD all other ingredients and simmer for 15 minutes.

SERVE browned side up, sprinkled with parsley and paprika.

Szechuan Glazed Duckling

SERVES 4 TO 6.

DUCKLING AND GLAZE:

1 Long Island duckling, approximately
    5 1/2 pounds

GLAZE:

1/3 cup sweet and sour stir-fry sauce

1/3 cup Korean teriyaki stir-fry sauce

1/3 cup Szechuan spicy stir-fry sauce

REMOVE giblets and set aside for sauce. The liver and heart may be used for paté.

REMOVE wings at second joint. Cut off neck skin. Set wing tips and neck skin aside with the giblets.

REMOVE and discard excess body fat.

RINSE duckling and pat dry with towel.

COMBINE glaze ingredients and massage into interior and exterior of duckling.

PLACE duckling in flat glass dish and let rest for 1 to 6 hours. (If you refrigerate duckling, remove it from the refrigerater for an hour before roasting.)

PREHEAT oven to 500°.

TRANSFER duckling to a foil-lined roasting pan. Set it on a roasting pedestal or raised rack.

PLACE duckling on the lowest rack in pre-heated oven. Immediately turn off the heat and *Resist Opening the Oven Door for 1 Hour.*

AFTER 1 HOUR, remove duckling from the oven, let rest for 5 minutes. Carve or cut up duckling into serving portions.

NAP with sauce *(recipe at right).*

SERVE duckling with Steamed Grains and Rices (page 134), Skagit Greens (page 119), and Carrots with Triple-sec (page 112).

DUCKLING SAUCE:

Neck, wing tips, giblets (except for liver and heart), and neck skin from 1 duckling

2 tablespoons extra-virgin olive oil

1/2 cup bourbon whiskey

1 1/2 cups Merlot wine

1 cup whipping cream

4 to 5 ounces hot jalapeno pepper jelly

1 tablespoon creamed horseradish sauce

IN A LARGE SKILLET, sauté duckling neck, giblets, wing tips, and neck skin on medium heat until browned, approximately 10 minutes.

REDUCE HEAT to low, cover pan tightly, and continue to cook for another 10 minutes or until giblets are tender.

DRAIN off drippings.

RETURN PAN TO HEAT. Pour whiskey over skillet ingredients, set alight carefully and let burn off completely.

ADD Merlot to pan and bring to a boil. Let simmer at medium heat until reduced by half.

REMOVE all solids from skillet, retaining the reduced liquids.

RETURN liquids in skillet to high heat. Add whipping cream, stirring constantly with a wooden spoon.

REDUCE until bubbles become quite small and a wooden spoon drawn slowly through the sauce leaves tracks.

ADD jalapeno jelly and stir until melted, then add horseradish.

SPOON sauce over or under carved duckling slices.

Rock Cornish Hens Stuffed With Rice Dressing

This is an old favorite from my own files.

SERVES 2 TO 4.

2 Rock Cornish hens

Salt and fresh ground pepper to taste

3 to 4 tablespoons of butter

1/2 cup celery, chopped

1 medium onion, chopped

1 cup mushrooms, chopped

1/4 cup green pepper, diced

2 cups cooked rice

1/2 cup ripe olives, chopped

2 to 3 tablespoons soy sauce

Melted butter for brushing over outside of hens

PREHEAT oven to 350°.

SPRINKLE the insides of hens with salt and pepper.

MELT butter in a skillet. Add celery, onions, mushrooms, and green pepper. Sauté until barely tender.

COMBINE sautéed vegetables with rice, olives, and soy sauce, mixing well and fill hen cavities with rice mixture.

BRUSH outside skin with melted butter, sprinkle with paprika, and a bit more salt and pepper.

PUT HENS in a roasting pan with a small amount of water. Bake for 1 hour at least or until done. It sometimes takes another 15 minutes. You can wrap the hens in foil to bake and open up the foil for the last 15 minutes to brown the skin. If you have more stuffing than will fit in the cavity, wrap up the extra in a piece of foil and bake alongside the hens.

Norwegian Game Hens With Gjetost Sauce

Kathi Babraitis of Burlington serves these delicious hens at her annual smorgasbord party to give her guests a little taste of Norway.

SERVES 6 AS MAIN-DISH OR 12 AS BUFFET.

6 Cornish game hens

1/2 medium lemon, quartered lengthwise

Salt and pepper

1/4 cup dry sherry

1/4 cup whipping cream

1/2 cup chicken stock

1 tablespoon red currant or sour cherry jelly

2 to 3 tablespoons (1/2 ounce) grated Norwegian *gjetost* cheese

1/2 teaspoon dry mustard

1/4 cup sour cream

Chopped fresh parsley for garnish

PREHEAT oven to 350°.

RUB hens inside and out with the cut side of the lemon quarters. Lightly sprinkle them inside and out with salt and pepper.

ARRANGE the hens in a single layer in two medium baking pans or one large pan. Roast for 1 hour or until juices run clear.

TRANSFER to platter and keep warm in oven while making sauce.

POUR pan juices into skillet, along with all baked-on bits.

COOK over high heat for 1 minute. Whisk in cream, sherry, and chicken stock and cook for 1 minute more, stirring constantly.

REDUCE heat to low and whisk in jelly, mustard, and cheese, stirring until smooth.

WHISK in butter and sour cream and just heat through. Taste for seasoning and correct if necessary.

TO SERVE, spoon some sauce over each hen and sprinkle with parsley. Pass remaining sauce in a bowl.

1988 SKAGIT CUISINE WINNER

Corn-Chili Rellenos

A favorite recipe from former county commissioner, Ruth Wylie of Fir Island.

SERVES 8

2 4-ounce cans whole green chilies

1/2 pound Monterey jack cheese, cut in strips

2 eggs, beaten slightly

3/4 cup evaporated milk

1 15-ounce can cream style corn

1/2 teaspoon salt

1 cup cheddar cheese, grated

PREHEAT oven to 350°.

SLIT chilies lengthwise and remove seeds.

STUFF generously with strips of jack cheese.

LAY stuffed chilies in a 9x13-inch baking dish.

IN MIXING BOWL, combine eggs, milk, corn, and salt. Blend well.

POUR mixture over chilies. Sprinkle with cheddar and bake for 30 minutes.

El Gitano Special Burritos

Adrian Ibarra, native of Mexico, came to the Skagit Valley in 1983. He and his wife Ruth own El Gitano, a Mexican restaurant on Fairhaven Avenue in Burlington which has been recognized for its fine food and spectacular Margaritas by the publishers of Northwest Best Places. *El Gitano serves everything from fried ice cream to their most popular burrito, "El Gitano Special."*

SERVES 6.

BURRITOS:

6 10-inch flour tortillas

2 1/2 cups refried beans

2 1/2 cups cooked rice

1 1/2 cups cheddar cheese, grated

Chopped fresh tomatoes, green onions, guacamole, or thinly sliced jalapenos for garnish

PREHEAT oven to 400°.

PLACE rice and beans in equal portions on center of tortillas and cover with ladle of meat sauce *(recipe on right)*.

ROLL each tortilla burrito-style and place in baking dish. Ladle more sauce over top of each and sprinkle with grated cheddar cheese.

BAKE until cheese melts. (Use microwave if you wish.)

REMOVE from oven. Spread light coat of guacamole over top and sprinkle with chopped tomatoes, green onions, and jalapenos to taste.

MEAT SAUCE:

4 pounds lean pork, leg or loin, cut into bite-sized chunks

2 green bell peppers, chopped

1 medium onion, chopped

1 teaspoon salt

1/2 teaspoon granulated garlic

1/4 teaspoon fresh ground pepper

Pinch of oregano

1/2 bunch cilantro

1/2 bunch green onions

3 pieces of celery, leaves included

1 to 3 jalapeno peppers

STEAM meat in a saucepan with 1/2-inch water until barely tender, about 10 minutes.

ADD peppers, yellow onion, and spices to meat and stir well.

WHILE meat mixture steams, place cilantro, green onions, celery, and jalapenos in blender with 1/4 cup water. Blend until it forms a green sauce. If sauce is thin, mix a teaspoon or more of cornstarch with enough cold water to make a smooth paste and stir into sauce.

POUR sauce into steaming meat mixture and simmer until meat is very tender, about 1/2 hour. Stir often to prevent meat from sticking to saucepan.

Chili Verde

Stephen Thornton, architectural designer-builder, is also a great cook. His savory Chili Verde is a prime example.

SERVES 6.

4 pounds pork roast

2-3 quarts stock—vegetable, chicken, or pork

CUT roast into spoon-sized pieces.

PLACE meat in large pot with stock, bring to a boil, skim off any foam, reduce heat to simmer.

SAUCE:

2 large onions, chopped

3-4 garlic cloves, minced

2 tablespoons olive oil

3 cinnamon sticks

2 tablespoons nutmeg

2 tablespoons ground coriander

4 whole cloves

1 cup canned salsa verde

3 7-ounce cans whole green chilis, sautéed

2 cups canned or fresh tomatillos, chopped

SAUTÉ onions and garlic in oil until onions are soft.

ADD remaining ingredients to onions and garlic. Reduce until slightly thickened, approximately 20 minutes.

ADD meat and stock. Bring to a boil, reduce heat, and simmer for 2 hours.

SERVE in bowls, with corn tortillas and condiments.

SUGGESTED CONDIMENTS:
Chopped green onions
Chopped tomatoes
Chopped cilantro
Grated cheese
Chopped radishes

Sour Cream Enchiladas

A versatile recipe for any season, one that can be made by eliminating the olives and using low-fat sour cream and cheeses.

SERVES 10.

8 10-inch flour tortillas

1 pint sour cream

1 8-ounce package shredded mozzarella cheese

1/4 cup flour

6 green onions, chopped

1 15-ounce can chili sauce without beans

1 15-ounce can mild enchilada sauce

1 7-ounce can chopped Ortega green chilies

1 2 1/4-ounce can chopped olives, drained

1 cup fresh mushrooms, chopped

1 generous cup of shredded cheddar cheese for topping

PREHEAT oven to 350°.

IN A BOWL, combine sour cream, mozzarella cheese, flour, onions, mushrooms, and green chilies.

MIX chili sauce and enchilada sauce in separate bowl. Pour half the mixture into 9x13 inch baking pan or casserole dish, covering the bottom.

SPOON sour cream-cheese mixture onto individual tortillas and roll them up.

PLACE enchiladas on top of sauce bed in casserole and pour remaining sauce over them.

COVER the sauced enchiladas with thick layer of cheddar cheese.

BAKE 30 to 45 minutes or until enchiladas are hot and bubbly.

German-Style Meatloaf

Bill Stendal, mayor of Sedro-Woolley, shares a favorite old family recipe.

SERVES 6.

1 1/2 pounds lean ground beef

1 cup dry bread crumbs

2 beaten eggs

1/4 cup milk

2 tablespoons onion, minced

1 teaspoon salt

1/4 teaspoon pepper

1/4 teaspoon dry mustard

ADD:

4 medium potatoes, cut in 1/4-inch slices

2 medium onions, cut in 1/4-inch slices

2 15-ounce cans tomato sauce

2 tablespoons sugar

1/2 cup catsup

3 strips fried bacon (optional)

COMBINE ingredients in mixing bowl with fork until well blended.

FORM mixture into a 6-inch round ball, place in a 12-inch skillet, and flatten top slightly.

BROWN on one side. Turn over using two spatulas.

IF USING BACON, wrap slices around meat loaf and secure in place with toothpick for an added touch.

ARRANGE potato and onion slices alternately around meat loaf.

ADD sugar to tomato sauce and catsup and pour over potatoes, onions, and meat loaf.

COVER skillet and simmer for 1 hour.

Anna Carlson's Potato Sausage

Potato sausage is a traditional Swedish dish served with lefse or Jamtland bread on Christmas Eve. Before starting, you will need to buy sausage casings from your butcher.

MAKES ABOUT 21 12-INCH SAUSAGES.

1/4 pound of Danish hog casings*

6 pounds lean ground beef

3 pounds pork sausage

9 pounds raw potatoes, peeled and ground in meat grinder

2 large onions, ground in meat grinder

Salt to taste

3 teaspoons powdered allspice

1 teaspoon fresh-ground pepper

2 packages dry onion soup mix

12 whole allspice

1 or 2 bay leaves

*If sold only by the pound, freeze the rest or have a sausage making party with friends.

NOTE: Sausage can be frozen and re-heated in an electric skillet with enough water to keep it moist. I add 6 to 8 whole allspice and a pinch of garlic powder to water for flavor.

MIX all ingredients, except casings, thoroughly in a large container.

SOAK casings in tepid water for 20 minutes prior to filling.

PUT one end of casing over the faucet and flush *gently* with water. Make sure your sink strainer is in, so that casing cannot be sucked down into the drain. Take care to keep casing from twisting around itself and tangling. Drain and cut casing into 18 to 24 inch lengths.

FILL casings using a funnel with a 3/4-inch opening at its narrowest point to 2 inches at the top. Push the casing as far up on funnel as you can without ripping it and hold firmly in place while pressing the meat mixture through the funnel opening into the casing. Leave enough room at each end to tie the two ends together to form a circular sausage. An inverted angel food cake pan can be used as a funnel.

TO COOK SAUSAGE:

FILL a large heavy pan with enough boiling water to cover sausage. An electric skillet works well.

ADD salt to taste, bay leaf or leaves, and whole allspice to boiling water.

PRICK sausages several times with a fork to prevent splitting, then add to boiling water. Simmer for 20 minutes.

WHILE SAUSAGE SIMMERS, cook the Jamtland bread or lefse *(pages 148 and 149)* on a greased griddle.

BUTTER the lefse and wrap it around the cooked sausage.

Swedish Meatballs

Spicy and flavorful, Swedish meatballs from the Valley's Scandinavian pioneers are a favorite the year around.

SERVES 6.

1 thick slice white bread

1/2 cup milk

3/4 pound twice-ground round beef

1/2 pound twice-ground veal

1/4 pound twice-ground pork

2 eggs, well beaten

1/4 cup onion, finely minced

1 tablespoon butter

3 tablespoons fresh parsley, chopped

1/4 teaspoon paprika

1/2 teaspoon lemon rind, grated

1 teaspoon lemon juice

1 teaspoon Worcestershire sauce

2 cups canned beef consommé

2 tablespoons flour

1 3-ounce can sliced mushrooms with liquid

PREPARE ground meats by grinding together twice or have your butcher do it for you.

SOAK bread in milk in small bowl.

ADD well-beaten eggs to meat mixture.

SAUTÉ onions in butter and add to meat mixture.

SQUEEZE liquid from bread and add it with rest of seasonings to meat mixture. Combine well and form into 1-inch meatballs.

BROWN meatballs in butter. Add consommé, cover and simmer until meatballs are cooked, about 15 minutes.

REMOVE meatballs and set aside. Thicken consommé sauce with flour. When smooth, add undrained mushrooms. Return meatballs to sauce and serve hot.

Wild Game Meatballs In Grape Chili Sauce

My grandson Bill Trueman tells me he only hunts for bear where there are no salmon to taint the meat's flavor. The grape-chili sauce reduces the often pungent game flavor.

SERVES 16 AS APPETIZER OR 8 AS ENTRÉE.

1 onion, chopped

2 sourdough English muffins, crumbled, or 3 slices sourdough bread

4 eggs, well beaten

1 pound bear sausage or Tarheel Pork Sausage

1 pound ground venison or ground veal

1 pound extra lean ground beef

1 tablespoon Worcestershire sauce

1/2 teaspoon Tobasco sauce

1 teaspoon salt

1/2 teaspoon fresh-ground pepper

1 teaspoon or less dried tarragon

PUT onion and bread in food processor and pulse until pulverized. Add eggs and meats and continue to process until all are blended well.

ADD seasonings and continue to whirl for another minute.

FORM mixture into 1-inch balls. Brown on all sides in hot oiled skillet.

NOTE: Always cook wild meat well enough to destroy any parasites that might cause trichinosis.

SAUCE:

1 12-ounce bottle Heinz Chili Sauce

1 10-ounce bottle grape jelly

COMBINE sauce and jelly in saucepan and heat on low until jelly melts.

POUR over meatballs and simmer on lowest heat for a few minutes before serving.

SERVE meatballs alone as appetizer or with rice or potatoes as main dish.

Cabbage Rolls

This traditional recipe is a Croatian specialty that takes time to prepare but is well worth the effort.

SERVES 10 TO 12.

1 large head cabbage

1 pound smoked ham hocks

1 1/2 pounds lean ground beef

1/2 pound smoked ham, ground

1/4 pound lean peppered bacon, chopped

1 cup raw rice

1/2 cup celery including leaves, chopped fine

1 clove garlic, minced

1 large onion, chopped

1 egg, lightly beaten

1 teaspoon paprika

Salt and pepper to taste

1 22-ounce can sauerkraut

1/2 cup onion, chopped for sauce layer

1 15-ounce can tomato sauce

PLACE ham hock in saucepan, cover with water, and bring to a boil, then simmer an hour or more. Save the broth.

WHILE HAM HOCK COOKS, core cabbage and place leaves in boiling water. As leaves wilt, remove carefully and place on paper towels to drain.

WHEN LEAVES ARE COOL enough to handle, remove thick vein.

COOK chopped bacon in skillet until crisp. Set bacon aside and drain off fat left in skillet, leaving 2 tablespoons.

ADD ground meats to skillet and brown slightly. Add 1/2 of onion, celery, and garlic. Cook until transparent.

STIR in rice, salt and pepper to taste, and half of tomato sauce. Stir in cooked bacon and beaten egg.

COARSE CHOP any cabbage not used for wrapping and place in bottom of heavy baking pan, preferably a Dutch oven.

RINSE and drain sauerkraut and layer over chopped cabbage.

TO FILL CABBAGE LEAVES:

PLACE approximately 1/4 to 1/3 cup of meat filling in center of each cabbage leaf. Fold edges to center and tuck in ends.

PLACE a single layer of rolls, seam side down, on sauerkraut in pan. Cover with another layer of sauerkraut. Repeat layers as necessary, finishing with a sauerkraut layer.

SPRINKLE with reserved 1/2 chopped onion. Cover with shredded ham hock meat.

SKIM fat off ham broth. Add enough ham broth to remaining tomato sauce to cover the cabbage rolls.

POUR sauce over rolls and bake in a 350° oven for 1 1/2 to 2 hours or simmer on top of stove. Delicious served with Croatian Cornmeal Cheese Bread *(page 151)*.

Beef Ragout (Haché)

William and Helen Roozen, founders of Washington Bulb Company, settled in the Skagit Valley in 1947 from Holland. Their originally small farm has now grown into the largest tulip, daffodil, and iris bulb-producing enterprise in the United States. On Beaver Marsh Road, the Roozens created the spectacular display garden called Roozengaarde, which is visited by thousands each spring. The following entrée is one of Helen Roozen's traditional Dutch recipes.

SERVES 4 TO 6.

2 pounds beef stew meat or leftover roast

1 large onion, chopped

1/4 cup butter

1/4 cup flour

3/4 teaspoon curry powder or to taste

2 cups leftover gravy or beef or chicken bouillon

Pepper, freshly ground

Bay leaf

8 whole cloves

6 small whole shallots

MELT butter in a large heavy pot or electric skillet and add onions.

COOK until onions are transparent. Add flour and curry powder. Continue to stir until lightly browned.

STIR in leftover gravy or bouillon, pepper, bay leaf, cloves, and shallots.

WITH HEAT ON LOW, simmer for 5 to 10 minutes before adding meat.

CUT meat into 1 1/4-inch squares. Add to gravy mixture and continue to simmer until meat is very tender, approximately 1 hour. Stir often enough to prevent sticking, adding more water as needed.

NOTE: The Roozens traditionally serve Haché *with potatoes. It is also good with pasta or rice.*

Beef Stew With Beer

This is a great winter dish. Add a green salad and hot crusty bread for a complete hearty meal.

SERVES 8.

4 pounds lean beef, cut into 1 to 1 1/2 inch cubes

1/4 cup olive oil

6 to 8 cloves garlic

3 tablespoons brown sugar

1/4 cup red wine vinegar

1/2 cup chopped parsley

2 teaspoons dried thyme

2 bay leaves

1 1/2 to 2 teaspoons salt

1/2 to 1 teaspoon freshly grated pepper

2 12-ounce cans beer

2 10-ounce cans beef broth

8 boiler size onions, peeled

8 carrots, cut into diagonal pieces

6 medium or 10 small potatoes, cut into chunks

Parsley, chopped for garnish

PREHEAT oven to 350°.

IN DUTCH OVEN or heavy roasting pan, heat oil to brown beef cubes. (You can roll the meat in flour first to seal in the juices and thicken the stew.)

WHEN ALL MEAT is browned, add rest of above ingredients. Cover and place in oven and let cook for 2 hours.

ADD onion, carrots, and potatoes. Cover again and cook until vegetables are tender. If stew appears dry as it cooks, add a little water.

Lamb Rack Chops Black Swan

Martin Hahn, chef of the Wild Iris Bed and Breakfast in LaConner, shares the following recipe for double-cut lamb rack chops in a crust. For many years, Martin was chef-owner of the Black Swan restaurant, a Northwest Best Places *favorite.*

SERVES 4.

SAUCE:

4 heads (clusters) of garlic or 2 ounces of pre-roasted garlic

1/2 ounce of Gorgonzola cheese

1/2 ounce dry Marsala

PREHEAT oven to 450°.

ROAST the whole garlic clusters in a sealed aluminum foil boat for 45 minutes.

OPEN foil boat, pour Marsala over garlic, sprinkle Gorgonzola on bottom of foil boat and roast for another 15 minutes or until garlic is very soft.

SQUEEZE garlic cloves out of their skins. Place in food processor with juices and residue from the bottom of foil boat, and blend. Set aside until lamb is cooked.

LAMB:

4 double-cut lamb rack chops (4 per half rack—shim removed)*

1/2 ounce Parmesan-Reggiano cheese

1/2 ounce bread crumbs

4 pinches cracked black pepper

4 sprigs fresh rosemary

1/4 cup olive oil

May need to special order from meat counter.

TRIM fat from rib chops.

IN A FOOD PROCESSOR combine cheese, cracked pepper, bread crumbs, and rosemary. Place mixture in flat bowl for breading chops.

RUB lamb chops with olive oil and roll them in breading mix, packing tightly.

PLACE lamb chops on parchment paper in roasting pan and roast for 18 minutes in pre-heated oven (medium-rare) or until done to taste.

LET ROASTED CHOPS REST about 10 minutes.

GARNISH:

Rosemary sprigs

Edible flowers—borage, nasturtiums, and violets

PLACE dollop of sauce on each serving plate; place one chop on top of sauce; set a sprig of rosemary between ribs of chop; and sprinkle edible flowers around plate.

Wine Recommendation: Hearty but fruity red such as Merlot from Columbia, Kiona, or Hogue Cellars; Pinot Noir from Duck Pond, Henry Estate, or Argyle.

Lamb Moussaka

SERVES 6 TO 8.

2 medium eggplants
1/2 cup margarine
4 tablespoons butter or margarine
4 medium onions, sliced
3 cloves garlic, crushed
1 pound ground lamb
3/4 teaspoon salt
1/2 teaspoon thyme
1/2 teaspoon oregano
1/2 cup canned tomatoes
1/2 cup dry white wine
2/3 cup parsley, chopped (optional)
2 eggs, separated
1 cup fresh bread crumbs
4 tablespoons flour
3 cups milk
1/4 teaspoon nutmeg
1/8 teaspoon cinnamon
1/8 teaspoon fresh ground pepper
1 cup parmesan cheese, freshly grated

PREHEAT oven to 350°.

CUT unpeeled eggplants into slices. Brown on both sides in 1/2 cup margarine, and set aside.

SAUTÉ onion and garlic in 2 tablespoons butter for 5 minutes. Add lamb and sauté until light brown.

ADD salt, tomatoes, wine, and parsley and simmer for 30 minutes.

COOL, then add stiffly beaten egg whites and 1/2 cup of the bread crumbs.

MAKE A WHITE SAUCE with remaining two tablespoons of butter, flour and milk.

BEAT egg yolks with nutmeg, cinnamon, and pepper. Stir into the white sauce very slowly. Simmer 2 minutes, stirring constantly.

SPRINKLE 1/4 cup bread crumbs over the bottom of a greased 4 quart casserole. Layer the eggplant slices, the meat mixture and the sauce. Repeat layers and finish with sauce on top. Sprinkle remaining crumbs and parmesan cheese over all.

BAKE for 1 hour.

Stuffed Pork Roast

Skagit Valley Finns serve this fruity Christmas treat year around.

SERVES 8.

1 pork boneless roast, 5 to 6 pounds
18 pitted prunes, chopped
2 cups onion, chopped
1 1/2 cups apple, peeled and chopped
1/4 cup applesauce
1 10 1/2-ounce can beef consommé

PREHEAT oven to 325°.

CUT deep cavity lengthwise in pork to make pocket for prune-apple mixture.

IN A BOWL, combine prunes with 1/2 chopped onion, all of apples, and applesauce.

PLACE mixture in cavity of roast. Over-lap meat edges and tie with string. If there is a layer of fat on meat, score it, then place pork fat-side up on bed of remaining chopped onions in roasting pan.

POUR consommé over top and bake for 30 to 35 minutes per pound, basting often with pan juices.

REMOVE meat from pan and keep warm.

SAUCE:
1 cup red currant jelly
1/2 cup orange juice
1/3 cup ruby port wine
Salt and pepper to taste

SKIM fat from pan liquids. Bring juices to a boil, making sure to scrape in the browned bits from bottom of pan. Re-duce by simmering for 5 to 10 minutes.

STIR in currant jelly, orange juice, wine, and seasonings. Simmer for 10 to 15 minutes.

AFTER REMOVING string from roast, slice thinly. Serve with a dribbling of sauce. The rest of sauce can be served in a gravy boat.

Rookery, Rock Sound

Seals barking.

Distant dogs across
afternoon expanses.

Stark weed,
the autumnal sun
setting…

Outboard powered
in-shore gillnet fishboats
strumming in
the evening chill coming
looming mind seine.

—Bill Slater

Barbecued Salmon

SERVES 12.

1 large filleted salmon

1/2 cup melted butter (can use part olive oil)

3 cloves crushed garlic

1 tablespoon lemon or lime juice

SEAR salmon, flesh side down, on a greased grill over hot coals.

TURN salmon skin side down and coat with combined butter, garlic, and lemon.

COOK until salmon flakes and serve with George Dunlap's barbecue sauce *(see below)*.

SAUCE:

A favorite from the Dunlap family in LaConner for barbecued salmon and other meats.

1/2 pound butter

1 clove garlic, minced

4 tablespoons soy sauce

2 tablespoons prepared mustard

1/4 to 1/2 cup catsup

Dash Worcestershire sauce

1 tablespoon olive oil (optional)

Dash of lemon juice (optional)

MIX all ingredients in a small saucepan and heat slowly on low. (If sauce heats too fast, it will curdle.)

COOL sauce and serve with salmon.

Baked Salmon À La Paul Heald

Artist Paul Heald, longtime summer resident on Pull and Be Damned Road near Hope Island, taught me how to bake salmon this way. Fresh sockeye is best.

SERVES 12.

1 large salmon, filleted
1 large white onion, sliced thin

SAUCE:
1/2 cup butter, melted
1/2 cup lite mayonnaise
1/4 cup lite soy sauce
1/2 teaspoon fresh-ground pepper
6 to 8 cloves garlic, crushed

PREHEAT oven to 400°.

MELT butter in a small saucepan.

WHISK in mayonnaise, soy sauce, and pepper. Add crushed garlic and combine well. Heat sauce until just warmed through.

LAY salmon fillets on cookie sheets with skin side down. Spread thin layer of sauce over fillets.

ARRANGE sliced onions across top and cover all with more sauce.

BAKE until fish flakes—from 20 minutes to 35 minutes, depending on the thickness of the fish.

NOTE: If there is any sauce left over, use it to baste during baking.

Baked Salmon
With Crab & Artichoke Sauce

This is Burlington resident Kathi Babraitis' 1988 Skagit Cuisine winning recipe.

SERVES 4.

BAKED SALMON:

4 salmon steaks, 1 inch thick and 4 to 6 ounces each

1 tablespoon olive oil

1 tablespoon lemon juice

Fresh parsley, chopped for garnish

PREHEAT oven to 450°.

MAKE sauce *(see below)*.

PLACE salmon steaks in 7x11 inch glass baking dish.

IN A SMALL BOWL, whisk olive oil and lemon juice. Brush both sides of salmon steaks with the mixture.

BAKE for 9 to 11 minutes or until salmon flakes easily.

TRANSFER salmon onto individual plates. Spoon sauce down center of each and garnish with parsley.

SAUCE:

1 1/2 teaspoons olive oil

1/4 cup green onions, chopped

3 garlic cloves, minced

3 tablespoons sweet red pepper, chopped

1 4-ounce can water packed artichoke hearts, chopped

2 tablespoons dry white wine

1 1/2 cups whipping cream

3/4 cup fresh crab meat or 1 6-ounce can crab meat

2 tablespoons Dijon mustard

Dash of hot pepper sauce

HEAT olive oil in a 10-inch skillet over medium heat.

ADD onion, garlic, and red pepper and cook 2 minutes. Do not brown.

ADD artichoke hearts and wine, and cook 1 minute or until wine is reduced by half.

ADD cream and, when it begins to bubble, add crab meat, mustard, and pepper sauce.

REDUCE heat to lowest setting and let sauce simmer while baking salmon. Stir occasionally.

1988 SKAGIT CUISINE WINNER

Salmon In Puff Pastry With Champagne Sauce

Kathi Babraitis said of this recipe, "Don't worry! It's so easy even my teenage niece could do it!"

SERVES 4.

4 salmon fillets, 4 ounces each

1/2 cup mushrooms, sliced

2 green onions, sliced

1 17 1/4-ounce package frozen puff pastry sheets

1 beaten egg for egg wash

PREHEAT oven to 425°.

LET the pastry stand at room temperature for 30 minutes to soften.

LIGHTLY FLOUR work board. Roll first sheet of pastry to about 10x14 inches, cut in half, and set aside. Repeat with second sheet of pastry, so that you have 4 5x7-inch pieces.

SET one salmon fillet in center of each pastry piece and divide the sliced mushrooms and green onions equally among the fillets.

BRUSH edges of pastry with egg wash, then fold pastry over salmon. Pinch edges to seal. (At this point you can cover with plastic wrap and hold in refrigerator for up to 6 hours.)

BRUSH pastry packets with egg wash. Refrigerate for 10 minutes.

BAKE for 20 to 25 minutes. If packets start to get too brown during cooking, place foil over them. They should be a beautiful golden brown when done. Remove from oven and keep warm while you make the sauce.

CHAMPAGNE SAUCE:

1/2 bottle of dry champagne

1/2 cup green onions, chopped, white part only

3 cups whipping cream

Salt and pepper to taste

REDUCE champagne and chopped onions over high heat to a glaze in the pan. This takes about 20 minutes.

ADD cream, mix well, and reduce until the sauce coats the back of a spoon.

SEASON with salt and pepper to taste.

POUR over salmon packets and serve.

Pickled Salmon

This recipe dates back to the turn of the century in LaConner. It was printed in a 1916 club cookbook, The Billiken Cookbook, *under the name of Mrs. C. J. Sewell. The original recipe called for: "One fine, fresh salmon cut into large pieces, boiled in salted water, as if for eating. Drain well and set in cool place until next day. Then make the pickle, which must be in proportion to the fish. To 1 quart of the water in which the fish was boiled allow 2 quarts of good vinegar, 1 ounce of black pepper, 1 nutmeg grated and a dozen blades of mace. Boil together in a kettle closely covered. Cool vinegar, pour over salmon, cover it closely, put in a cool, dry place and it will keep for many months."*

MAKES APPROXIMATELY 2 QUARTS.

1 salmon, 4 to 5 pounds

1 1/2 quarts water

1 teaspoon salt

1 teaspoon dried onion flakes

1 teaspoon fresh grated nutmeg

1/2 teaspoon Dona Flora lemon pepper*

1/4 teaspoon mace

1/2 cup brown sugar

1 teaspoon gourmet peppercorns

3 cups apple cider vinegar

1 cup Hot and Spicy Dona Flora vinegar, or add a hot pepper to red wine vinegar

1 medium white onion, sliced thin

*Available at Skagit Valley Co-op and Snowgoose Produce. See page 13 for local Dona Flora products

REMOVE fins and tail from cleaned fish and cut into 3-inch chunks.

PLACE water in a spaghetti cooker or fish poacher and bring to a boil.

PLACE fish chunks in steamer above boiling water and turn heat to low. Simmer for 5 to 10 minutes or until fish will barely flake.

REMOVE fish from steamer and set aside to cool. Reserve cooking liquid for brine.

COMBINE 2 cups reserved fish liquor with the rest of the ingredients in a covered saucepan and heat to boiling point. Turn heat down and simmer for one minute. Set aside to cool.

PEEL skin from the cooled fish. Remove backbone, cartilage, and excess fat. Scrape off gray flesh with a dull knife and use tweezers to pull out any bones that are left.

CUT salmon into 1 1/2-inch chunks and layer in bowl with onion. Pour cooled, strained vinegar over top and refrigerate until served.

Halibut Pretending To Be Lobster

The following recipes were gleaned from one of my fishermen relatives. A commercial fisherman, Gary cooks seafood often. These two halibut recipes came from the fishing boat Reality.

SERVE 6 TO 8.

4 to 6 cups halibut, cut in 1-inch chunks

1 gallon water

3/4 cup sugar

1/4 cup salt

Juice of 2 to 3 fresh lemons

1/2 to 1 cup melted butter

RINSE fish and dry with paper towel.

BRING WATER to a boil in large pot. Add sugar and salt, stirring until dissolved.

TURN HEAT DOWN to simmer. When water stops boiling, add fish chunks, a cupful at a time. Allow to cook 3 to 4 minutes.

GENTLY REMOVE fish with slotted spoon and transfer to warm platter or chafing dish.

SERVE cooked fish chunks with combined lemon juice and melted butter for dipping.

Halibut Cooked In Beer Batter

SERVES 6 TO 8.

1 cup flour

1 cup pancake mix

1/2 cup cornmeal

2 eggs

1 teaspoon salt

1 can of beer

4 cups halibut, cut in 1-inch chunks

1 cup flour seasoned with pinch of garlic powder, pepper, and paprika

1 cup oil for deep-fat frying (or 1/4 cup for pan frying)

PLACE all ingredients, except halibut and seasoned flour, in a bowl and mix well.

PAT halibut chunks dry with paper towels and roll in seasoned flour. Shake off excess.

DIP floured pieces in batter and deep-fry until browned, about 2 to 3 minutes or pan fry until browned.

DRAIN on paper towels. Serve hot with lemon or condiments of your choice.

Clam Fritters

The sandy margins of the Valley are "clam country" where families can dig their own dinner.

SERVES 6.

1 quart fresh butter clams
3 eggs
1/2 stick soda crackers, crumbled
Fresh-ground pepper and salt to taste
1 small onion, chopped fine

GRIND cleaned clams using coarse blade.

IN A BOWL, combine clams, eggs, cracker crumbs, seasonings, and onion.

DROP fritter batter by large spoonfuls on hot oiled griddle or skillet and cook until browned, turn over and brown other side.

SERVE immediately.

Butter Clams Fried On The Half Shell

Another favorite cooking method after a successful clam-digging expedition.

SERVES 6 TO 8.

2 dozen fresh butter clams, about 3 inches long
2 eggs, whisked lightly
2 tablespoons water
1 cup Bisquick or seasoned flour, more if needed
Fresh-ground pepper and salt to taste
2 tablespoons vegetable oil for frying

COVER fresh clams with cold water and sprinkle handful of cornmeal over the top. Let sit for an hour or two.

RINSE clams in more cold water and scrub shells.

INSERT a sharp, thin knife at muscle hinge and cut each clam in half.

REMOVE the black tip of the neck.

DIP open side of clam in egg whisked with water.

DIP egged surface in flour, shake off excess, and sprinkle with seasonings.

HEAT oil in skillet and fry clams, battered side down, until golden brown and crisp, about 3 to 5 minutes.

Steamed Clams, Scallops, Or Mussels

SERVES 1 TO 2.

2 tablespoons butter

1 tablespoon shallots, chopped

1 clove garlic

1 sprig fresh thyme

2 tablespoons parsley, chopped

1 bay leaf

1/3 cup white wine (for scallops, use a little more wine or water)

1 pound cleaned clams, pink scallops, or mussels *(See Note)*

PLACE all ingredients in deep saucepan and steam over medium-high heat until all shells are open.

NOTE: CLEANING FRESH MUSSELS

WASH under cold running water.

SCRUB shells with a vegetable brush.

Remove barnacles with a small flat blade knife.

PULL off beards.

DISCARD any open or cracked shells.

PLACE cleaned fresh mussels (or clams) in a container of cold water. Sprinkle a handful of cornmeal over them and let sit for an hour. (This is said to help clean out the stomachs of shellfish.)

Tore's Flamed Seafood

Skagit Valley artist Guy Anderson recommends restaurateur Tore Dybfest as his favorite recipe: "If you want good food, talk to him." Dybfest, owner of the Lighthouse Inn, has created and cooked gourmet dishes for Anderson and other artists, including Mark Tobey, since the 1970s.

SERVES 4.

16 to 24 tiny new potatoes

3 to 4 chopped shallots

1 cup mushrooms, sliced

2 tablespoons butter or olive oil

1/2 cup white wine

3/4 cup whipping cream

1 teaspoon Old Bay seasoning

1/4 teaspoon fresh-ground pepper

1 1/2 cups raw, shelled and deveined large shrimp or prawns

1 1/2 cups raw bay scallops

1 cup freshly shelled new peas

1 cup fresh-cooked and shelled Dungeness crab

4 small Petrale sole fillets

1/2 cup brandy for flaming

PRE-STEAM potatoes for about 4 minutes.

IN A HEAVY SKILLET, sauté shallots and mushrooms in butter or olive oil.

ADD white wine, cream, and seasonings and simmer until reduced to the point that a wooden spoon drawn through it leaves tracks. Adjust seasonings if necessary. Add shrimp, sea scallops, potatoes, and peas, and simmer until shrimp turn pink. Add crab and cook another minute.

IN SECOND SKILLET, cook sole in butter. Place browned sole filets in center of seafood skillet, arranging vegetables and seafood around them.

PLACE slightly warmed brandy in large, long-handled stainless steel dipper and light. Pour flaming brandy over contents of seafood skillet and let burn off. Serve with rice pilaf.

Hot Steamed Crab In Oyster Sauce, Mandarin Style

Skagit Valley artist Richard Gilkey has a fondness for steamed cracked crab in oyster sauce, served over Chinese soft egg noodles. He claims the Tai Tung Cantonese restaurant in Seattle prepares it the way he likes it. Here is a version of the sauce based on my memory of its flavorful bouquet.

SERVES 2.

OYSTER SAUCE:

1 tablespoon light olive oil, or butter

6 to 8 Shiitake mushrooms, halved or quartered

2 tablespoons dry sherry or rice wine

2 cups defatted chicken broth

1/2 teaspoon ground white pepper

2 tablespoons cornstarch

1/4 cup water

5 tablespoons bottled oyster sauce

1/2 teaspoon sugar

1 teaspoon fresh ginger, grated

HEAT olive oil or butter in heavy saucepan on medium-high heat and add mushrooms. Sauté 2 minutes.

ADD sherry or wine and cook another 2 minutes.

TURN heat down to medium and add chicken broth and pepper.

IN A SMALL BOWL, blend cornstarch with water until smooth and stir into sauce.

ADD oyster sauce, sugar, and ginger. Continue to stir until sauce is thickened and smooth.

REMOVE sauce from heat, add cracked crab *(recipe follows)*, and pour over hot cooked noodles. At Tai Tung they serve this dish with the crab shell placed on top and with an accompanying bowl of steamed white rice.

STEAMED DUNGENESS CRAB:

These directions are courtesy of Blau Oyster Company, Samish Island.

SELECT GENEROUS-SIZED POT and fill to about half with cold water. Place on high heat. Add at least 1 cup of salt per gallon of water. Optional: add favorite herbs and spices.

AT ROLLING BOIL, add live crab and cover pot. When re-boil occurs, turn down heat and note time. Boil lightly for 15 minutes. Due to salt and seasonings, a messy boil-over is likely; maintain a light boil and be prepared. Cool crab by adding cold water to pot. Clean crab as soon as possible. Serve warm or chilled.

Blau's Basic Pan-Fried Oysters

Paul Blau is a third-generation owner of the Blau Oyster Company on Samish Island. Valley cooks often head to Blaus for fresh oysters and other seafood.

SERVES 4.

2 eggs

1 cup milk

2 cups (total) cracker meal, crushed saltines, and/or bread crumbs

4 tablespoons flour

Salt and pepper to taste

1 quart fresh-shucked oysters

Vegetable oil

BEAT together eggs and milk.

THOROUGHLY MIX cracker meal and/or bread crumbs with flour, salt and pepper to taste.

DIP oysters in egg and milk and roll in crumb mixture.

FRY in hot oil until cooked as desired. Well-done oysters will be golden to medium-brown.

Elizabeth Blau's Baked Oysters

SERVES 8 TO 10.

2 quarts oysters

8 ounces half-and-half

2 sticks soda crackers

1/2 stick butter (or more, to taste)

PREHEAT oven to 350°.

GREASE shallow baking pan.

IN A SAUCEPAN, blanch oysters in their juice.

CHOP oysters into bite-sized pieces.

CRUSH crackers into baking pan, layer with oysters and more crackers.

POUR half-and-half over oysters, covering bottom of pan.

DOT with butter; sprinkle with salt and pepper. (Optional: light sprinkle of nutmeg).

BAKE 30 minutes or until crackers brown.

Barbecued Oyster Sauce

Sid Stapleton of Samish Island grilled several bags of fresh oysters for an art opening at the Edison Eye Gallery recently. Each plateful disappeared within minutes of being placed on the buffet table. Here is the sauce he used to baste the oysters.

MAKES 1 QUART PLUS.

1 quart olive oil

1/2 cup dried oregano

1/4 cup dried basil

1 whole head of garlic cloves, crushed

1 teaspoon salt

Fresh-ground pepper to taste

1 tablespoon dried Habanero peppers

4 to 5 bay leaves

COMBINE all ingredients and let sit for 2 hours in covered container before using.

FOLLOW directions below for grilling oysters in shells. As soon as they can be opened, start basting oysters in cupped half of shells with a dribbling of sauce.

Blau's Barbecued Oysters In-The-Shell

SERVE MINIMUM OF 3 OYSTERS PER PERSON.

SET GRILL 1 foot above bed of HOT coals.

PLACE oysters on grill cupped side down, so liquid is retained.

MANY OYSTERS will open after cooking a few minutes. When this happens, or after 10 minutes, put on insulated mittens and begin prodding between the shells with a sharp instrument—oyster knife, rigid butter knife, or screw driver.

OYSTERS that firmly refuse to open should be allowed to cook longer. Those that open on their own or when only a little force is applied may be eaten immediately.

IF YOU CAN WAIT, and prefer more thoroughly cooked oysters, place or leave meats in cupped shells, add melted butter and seasoning of choice. Continue cooking until you can't resist any longer. Serve oysters right off grill with dipping sauce made of melted butter and generous portion of crushed garlic.

Blau Oyster Stew

MAKES 4 SERVINGS PER QUART OYSTERS.

1 quart oysters*

1 tablespoon butter (or more) per quart oysters

1 pint milk per quart oysters (skim, 2%, whole, or half-and-half)

Salt and pepper to taste

*Any size or grade will do, cut large oysters in bite-sized pieces.

PLACE whole or cut-up oysters in a saucepan, add butter, and sauté until the edges curl. Time is not critical: better to make sure they're done. Pacific oysters are hard to overcook.

ADD milk, salt, pepper, and other seasonings to taste.

HEAT to just below boiling point.

STEW may be thickened with cornstarch or instant mashed potatoes, if desired.

Oyster-Spinach Casserole

This is Fir Island artist John Simon's specialty. He warns that it is only for those who need cholesterol.

SERVES 6.

2 10-ounce boxes frozen spinach

2 cups cheddar cheese, cubed

2 cups cottage cheese

3 eggs, beaten

1/4 cup flour mix, such as Bisquick

6 to 8 oysters, chopped

PREHEAT oven to 350°.

MIX all ingredients together in bowl and pour into oiled baking dish.

BAKE for 1 1/2 hours.

Oyster Stew

SERVES 2.

1/2 cup mushrooms, sliced
2 tablespoons butter
1/2 stalk celery, chopped fine
1/2 pint fresh small oysters
2 medium potatoes, peeled and diced
1 cup half-and-half
Salt and fresh-ground pepper to taste

SAUTÉ mushrooms in butter for 2 to 3 minutes; stir in celery, and cook another 2 minutes.

ADD oysters and their liquid.

SIMMER until oyster edges begin to curl.

COVER potatoes with water in saucepan. Bring to a boil and simmer until potatoes are crunchy tender.

DRAIN off all but 1/2 cup of potato water. Add oyster mixture to potatoes in the saucepan.

ADD half-and-half, salt, and pepper.

HEAT and serve in soup bowls. For a complete meal, add green salad and French bread.

Pickled Shrimp

A main attraction at Skagit Valley smorgasbords.

SERVES 8 TO 10.

3 cups water

1/4 cup pickling spices, in a cheesecloth bag

1/4 cup celery leaves

2 teaspoons salt

2 pounds frozen or fresh uncooked medium shrimp, shelled and deveined

1 medium red onion, sliced and separated into rings

3 large or 6 small bay leaves

1 cup salad oil

1/3 cup tarragon vinegar

1 teaspoon celery seeds

1 teaspoon salt

2 tablespoons capers, drained

COMBINE water, bag of spices, celery leaves, and salt in large saucepan.

BRING TO A BOIL and add shrimp. Cook frozen shrimp according to package directions. If using fresh shrimp, reduce heat to medium after water comes to a boil and cook about 5 minutes or until pink.

DRAIN shrimp and place in large bowl with onion and bay leaves.

BEAT oil, vinegar, celery seeds, and salt in small bowl. Pour over shrimp and add capers. Toss gently.

COVER and refrigerate at least 2 days.

PLACE in a glass bowl and serve with toothpicks.

Pickled Oysters

SERVES 12.

2 dozen fresh oysters with liquid

1 large sweet white or red onion, thinly sliced

1/2 lemon, thinly sliced

1/4 teaspoon dry mustard

1 bay leaf

6 to 8 peppercorns

1/4 cup white wine vinegar

IN A SAUCEPAN, heat oysters in their own liquid until the edges curl.

REMOVE oysters from liquid with a slotted spoon and set aside.

ADD the rest of the ingredients to liquid and bring to a boil. Simmer for 30 seconds.

REMOVE from heat and strain, reserving onions and liquid.

POUR strained liquid over oysters. Add reserved onions.

CHILL for at least 2 hours before serving.

SKAGIT VALLEY FARE : ENTRÉES

The Teacher, Maggie Wilder

VEGETABLES

SQUASH

When I went to India
my guru said *squash*.

So I came home, learned
my neighbor's handle
and traded an old car for a plot of ground.

Stan was his name, or *Stosh*.
He said for your dead-beat Chevy
you get one season.

I dug and I hoed
and dropped the seeds in rows.

I planted crookneck, hubbard and spaghetti;
I planted the colorful turban,
the acorn, butternut and pattypan.
They were my village, and to keep it democratic,
next to the exotic delicata
I planted a family of zucchini.

Now the growing season's almost done
and old Stan complains his Chevy won't start.

Each crisp morning, when I hear him cranking,
I climb to my window and look out over
the unruly jumble of squash shape and squash color
arriving in the sun,

and have all I need: a life
of the spirit, and art.

—JAMES BERTOLINO

Sautéed Chanterelles With Mint & Peas

Retired school teacher Betty Crippen has lived in the Skagit Valley for many years, and she finds her own fresh mushrooms in secret wooded haunts. On occasion, she lets someone go along to find morels, but no one has yet pried out of her where she finds the elusive chanterelles.

SERVES 6.

1/2 pound chanterelle mushrooms, sliced

1/3 cup olive oil

1 pound small white mushrooms, sliced

3 1/2 cups fresh or frozen peas

1/4 to 1/2 cup fresh mint leaves

1 teaspoon salt

1 teaspoon fresh-ground pepper

HEAT oil in heavy skillet. Add mushrooms and sauté until lightly browned.

ADD peas and sauté 5 minutes. Add mint and seasonings, and serve.

Carrots With Triple-Sec

SERVES 4 TO 6.

6 to 7 fresh young carrots
1/2 cup white Zinfandel wine
2 tablespoons Triple-sec
1 tablespoon butter
Pinch of nutmeg

SCRAPE, rather than peel, carrots. Holding a sharp knife at a slight angle, cut into oblique rounds, approximately 1/4-inch thick.

IN A SAUCEPAN, over medium-high heat, stir carrots and wine until carrots are tender-crisp, and wine is reduced to a glaze, about 5 minutes.

DRIBBLE Triple-sec over cooked carrots. Stir and cook 3 or 4 minutes to evaporate alcohol.

JUST BEFORE SERVING, add butter and pinch of nutmeg. *(Butter adds sheen to carrots and holds glaze.)*

Zucchini Ratatouille

Clayton James is one of the Valley's treasured artists. A master sculptor and painter, he is also a good cook. The following recipe that he and wife Barbara brought to our latest potluck disappeared too fast for everyone to taste. Those who did said it was fantastic.

SERVES 4.

5 6-inch zucchini

1 jalapeno pepper, finely chopped

3 cloves garlic, minced

1 28-ounce can tomatoes, crushed

or 4 cups fresh-chopped tomatoes, seeds removed

1 large onion, chopped

1/2 large red bell pepper, chunk chopped

1/2 large yellow bell pepper, chunk chopped

2 tablespoons olive oil or more, if needed

Small bunch each fresh basil and fresh parsley, finely chopped, to taste

Grated cheese for topping

PREHEAT oven to 350°.

SLICE zucchini lengthwise into 1/4-inch thick pieces. Salt and let drain for 1/2 hour. Dry on towels.

ADD jalapeno and garlic to tomatoes in saucepan and cook over low heat for 30 minutes or until reduced to nicely thickened sauce.

IN A LARGE SKILLET, sauté onion and peppers in 1 tablespoon of olive oil until slightly softened, about five minutes. Add to tomato sauce along with basil and parsley.

SAUTÉ zucchini in remaining 1 tablespoon olive oil until browned on both sides.

LAYER zucchini and sauce alternately in 9-inch casserole. Top with grated cheese and bake covered for 20 minutes or until juice bubbles.

UNCOVER and bake for 10 minutes, or until cheese browns. Serve hot, cold, or at room temperature accompanied by black olives, crusty French bread, and green salad.

Roquefort Tomato Soufflé

From Thais and Howard Armstrong of Samish Island comes this savory vegetarian soufflé.

SERVES 4.

2 tablespoons butter

3 tablespoons flour

1 bay leaf

3/4 cup milk

1 whole clove

4 sprigs parsley

4 thin slices onion

Pinch of powdered dill

1/2 cup tomato juice

6 ounces Roquefort cheese

Pinch of salt and dash of pepper

4 eggs, separated

1/2 teaspoon salt

1/4 teaspoon dry mustard or curry powder

PREHEAT oven to 400°.

IN MEDIUM SAUCEPAN, melt butter and stir in flour. Heat until frothy and bubbly.

IN ANOTHER SAUCEPAN, place milk, bay leaf, clove, parsley, onion, and dill. Heat until milk is scalded. Strain and stir into hot butter-flour mixture.

ADD tomato juice and cook, stirring until sauce bubbles and thickens.

ADD crumbled cheese and stir until smooth. Season to taste with salt and pepper.

REMOVE sauce from heat and quickly beat in egg yolks.

BEAT egg whites with 1/2 teaspoon salt until stiff. Gently fold beaten egg whites and dry mustard into sauce. Pour into buttered and floured 1-quart soufflé dish.

BAKE for 20 to 25 minutes, or until soufflé is well-puffed and brown on top. Serve immediately.

Corn Cakes

Artist Bill Slater is known for his hearty corn cakes which he cooks for special breakfasts. Skagit Valley Co-op or a similar store carries whole dried corn.

SERVES 4.

1 cup whole dried corn

1 tablespoon light olive oil

1/4 cup powdered milk

1/2 to 1 teaspoon salt

1/4 teaspoon pepper

1/3 cup green onions, chopped

1/3 cup celery, chopped

1/4 cup fresh parsley, chopped

1 clove garlic, slivered

1/2 cup boiling water or slightly more if needed

Cheddar cheese slices

HEAT oil in a heavy skillet. Add corn and stir continually over medium heat until it smells richly of corn, about 10 minutes. Don't overcook.

REMOVE corn from heat and grind in grinder or food processor.

TRANSFER ground corn to mixing bowl. Add powdered milk, seasonings, and vegetables. Stir well.

STIR in boiling water to make a medium batter.

SHAPE corn cakes and fry in hot-oiled skillet until golden brown. Turn over and place slice of cheese on each cake.

LOWER heat and cook until cheese is melted.

Baked Onions Stuffed With Gruyère Cheese

SERVES 4.

4 large, sweet onions (such as Walla Walla sweets), peeled

8 green onions

1 bunch fresh herbs, such as sweet basil, tarragon and/or thyme

3/4 cup Gruyère cheese, grated

1/2 cup bread crumbs

PREHEAT oven to 350°.

BLANCH onions for 2 minutes in boiling water.

COOL slightly. Remove the centers and fine-chop centers along with the green onions and fresh herbs.

COMBINE chopped onions and herbs with 1/2 cup of cheese in a bowl and mix well.

PLACE onion shells in a buttered flat casserole dish. Fill with onion-herb-cheese mixture.

COMBINE remaining cheese with bread crumbs and sprinkle over onions. Bake for 30 minutes or until onions are tender and cheese is melted.

Glazed Onions

This simple and unusual recipe comes from a small cookbook produced by Morry and Florence Ekstrand, the parents of Skagit Valley resident Chris Molesworth.

SERVE 4 TO 6.

1 pound small white onions, peeled

1 tablespoon sugar

1 teaspoon salt

2 tablespoons butter

1 cup beef bouillon

PLACE onions in a heavy skillet.

SPRINKLE with sugar and salt.

ADD butter and bouillon.

SIMMER until bouillon has been absorbed.

COOK, in skillet over low heat, stirring often, until onions are golden brown and glazed.

SERVE as a side dish.

Spinach & Potato-Stuffed Onions

A favorite recipe from a Skagit Valley Co-op cooking class taught by Marie-Paule Braule.

SERVES 4.

4 large yellow sweet onions

1 cup fresh spinach, coarsely chopped

2 medium potatoes

2 tablespoons butter

1/4 cup whipping cream

1/4 teaspoon nutmeg

Salt and white pepper to taste

2 tablespoons parmesan cheese, freshly grated

PREHEAT oven to 400°.

PEEL onions and cut an X in the root end of each.

COOK in boiling water until just tender. Drain and cool.

SLICE OFF onion tops, and carefully remove the insides, leaving a double layer of onion. Save insides to use another time.

IN A STEAMER, blanch spinach until tender but still bright green. Drain and set aside.

PEEL potatoes and cut into eighths.

COOK in salted water until tender. Drain and mash.

BEAT butter, cream, and nutmeg into potatoes and fold in spinach. Add salt and pepper to taste and more cream if too dry.

SPOON mixture into onion shells, mounding the filling high.

PLACE in baking dish and sprinkle with cheese. Bake until tops are golden, about 20 minutes.

Skagit Greens, Southern Style

Wild greens were a staple for the Tarheel settlers from North Carolina. This recipe is suitable for wild greens such as young unsprayed dandelion leaves, lambs quarter, or stinging nettles (handle with gloves until cooked and pick only the new growth in spring) or spinach, chard, collards, turnip greens, mustard greens, or a mixture of any or all.

SERVES 4.

7 to 8 cups greens, coarsely chopped

4 slices lean bacon, chopped

2 tablespoons butter, olive oil or bacon drippings

1 large onion, chopped

2 cloves garlic, thinly sliced

1/3 cup vinegar

1 tablespoon honey

Salt and pepper to taste

Toasted pine nuts (optional)

WASH greens. Remove coarse stems and pat dry before measuring and setting aside.

COOK bacon until crisp and set aside to drain on paper towels.

OVER MEDIUM HEAT, in large non-reactive frying pan, sauté onion in fat for 1 minute. Add garlic and cook another minute. Add vinegar, honey, and seasonings and continue to cook until honey melts.

ADD greens. Toss and continue to cook until barely tender but still bright green.

ADD chopped bacon and pine nuts (if desired) and serve.

Vegetable Stir Fry In Ginger Sauce

Stir-frying, an ancient Oriental method of cooking, is quick and healthy. Beverly Swanson of the Skagit Valley Co-op says the secret of a good stir-fry is searing heat and keeping foods moving so they cook quickly. Use a wok or heavy skillet and a wooden spoon.

SERVES 4 TO 6.

3 tablespoons sesame oil

1 to 2 cloves garlic, minced

4 green onions, chopped

1 pound firm tofu, drained and cubed

8 cups mixed (preferably organic) vegetables sliced into thin, bite-sized pieces.*

CHOOSE ANY OF THE FOLLOWING OR COOK'S CHOICE:

Broccoli, mushrooms (Shiitake or other)

Cauliflower, zucchini, or yellow squash

Carrots, snow peas, green beans

Celery, bean sprouts

Green, red, or yellow sweet peppers

Greens: bok choy, Napa cabbage, spinach, or kale

1 tablespoon fresh ginger, grated

1/2 cup water

2 tablespoons Tamari soy sauce

3 tablespoons arrowroot or kuzu

Cut vegetable slices diagonally to expose more surface.

HEAT 2 tablespoons of oil in wok until a drop of water sizzles on contact.

SAUTÉ garlic and onions until translucent.

ADD firm, longer-cooking vegetables first. Keep them moving so they can cook quickly.

ADD the softer, faster-cooking vegetables. Leafy greens should be added last.

ADD tofu and keep mixture moving.

ADD water, tamari sauce, ginger, 1 tablespoon oil, and arrowroot.

COOK just until sauce turns thick, about 5 minutes.

SERVE stir-fry over brown rice, other whole grains, or pasta.

Down-On-The-Farm Vegetables

A local recipe handed from friend to friend to friend, leaving its origin in doubt.

SERVE 6 TO 8.

1 10 3/4 ounce can cream of chicken
   soup
1 cup sour cream or plain yogurt
1 cup shredded or thin-sliced carrots
2 pounds zucchini, sliced in rounds
1/2 cup onion, chopped
1 7 1/2-ounce package herb-seasoned
   stuffing mix
1/2 cup melted butter or margarine

PREHEAT oven to 350°.

COMBINE soup and sour cream in bowl and stir in carrots.

FOLD in zucchini and onion.

TOSS stuffing mix with melted butter and spread half of the mixture in bottom of 9x13-inch baking dish.

SPOON combined vegetables on top and sprinkle with remaining stuffing mix. Bake for about 40 minutes or until top is golden and crisp.

Lavone's Bean Casserole

Some people inherit money. I inherited bean seed. My mother brought a bag of lima-like bean seed from Kansas when we moved to the Skagit Valley in 1941, and she saved seed from those large, brightly colored beans every year. Now I grow them every year, saving enough seed for next year's planting plus enough to share with friends. This is a stellar potluck dish.

SERVES 12 TO 16.

3 quarts cooked large lima-type beans with 1 cup of their liquid

3 8-ounce cans vacuum-packed whole kernel corn or 3 cups fresh corn kernels

2 3/4 cups medium cheddar cheese, grated

1/2 teaspoon dried oregano

1/2 teaspoon dried thyme

1/2 teaspoon dried basil

PREHEAT oven to 400°.

PLACE beans in large casserole with liquid.

BAKE beans for 20 minutes (10 minutes for commercially canned beans).

ADD corn, 2 cups cheese, and herbs, Stir well.

REDUCE oven temperature to 375°. Bake casserole for another 15 minutes.

SPRINKLE on remaining cheese. Bake 15 to 20 minutes longer, or until cheese topping becomes crusty and light golden brown.

Potato Pancakes With Applesauce

A recent visitor from Berlin, Sabine Hoffman, cooked this traditional German potato pancake for a special treat. Good served for breakfast or as a dinner side dish.

MAKES 2 12-INCH PANCAKES.

3 medium baking potatoes

1 egg

2 tablespoons onion, finely grated

2 1/2 to 3 tablespoons flour

1/2 teaspoon salt

1/4 cup oil (or less, to taste)

1 to 1 1/2 cups applesauce (fresh if possible)

PEEL potatoes and drop in cold water until ready to grate.

IN MIXING BOWL, beat egg slightly. Add grated onion and gradually beat in flour and salt.

ONE AT A TIME, pat potatoes dry and grate coarsely into colander. Squeeze as much moisture as possible out of grated potato.

IMMEDIATELY STIR potato into egg batter and mix well. Repeat process for remaining potatoes.

IN HEAVY 12-INCH SKILLET or electric fry pan, heat oil quickly until it splutters. The more oil you use, the crisper the potato cake.

POUR one half of batter into hot skillet and flatten out with spatula to cover the skillet evenly.

COOK over medium high heat for a couple of minutes on each side. Pancakes should be dark golden brown and crisp around edges. You may need to add more oil to skillet for each new pancake.

SERVE as soon after cooking as possible with applesauce. Freshly made warm applesauce is best. *(See page 144 for a quick version.)*

Sinful Potatoes

SERVES 12.

2 quarts potatoes, peeled and sliced

2 bay leaves

1/4 cup butter

1/4 cup green onions, chopped

1 10 3/4-ounce can cream of chicken soup

1 cup sour cream

1/2 to 1 teaspoon salt

1/2 teaspoon fresh-ground pepper

1 cup cheddar cheese, grated, plus

1/3 cup or more cheddar for topping

PREHEAT oven to 350°.

PARBOIL potatoes with bay leaves until almost tender.

REMOVE bay leaves and drain potatoes.

ARRANGE potatoes in a 9x13-inch baking pan.

IN A SMALL SKILLET, melt butter and sauté onions till transparent.

REMOVE from heat. Add soup, sour cream, salt and fresh-ground pepper to taste, and 1 cup cheese. Pour mixture over potatoes, sprinkle with extra cheese, and bake for about 30 minutes, or until tender when tested with fork.

Quick Sweet & Sour Red Cabbage

Beth Hailey, known professionally as Dona Flora, has a multi-faceted flower and herb business. One of the Valley's many organic gardeners, she produces herbal vinegars and olive oils, some of which are used in this colorful recipe. Dona Flora products are available at Skagit Valley Co-op, Snow Goose Produce, and Saturday markets.

SERVES 8.

1 medium red cabbage, sliced thinly

1 large onion, diced

1 tart apple (such as Granny Smith), sliced

2 tablespoons of Dona Flora Hot & Spicy Olive Oil

1/4 cup Hot & Spicy Dona Flora Vinegar

2 tablespoons honey

Generous pinch of Dona Flora Lemon Pepper

Salt or soy sauce to taste

IN A LARGE FRYING PAN, cook vegetables and apple in olive oil until tender crisp.

STIR in vinegar, honey, and seasonings.

SERVE hot.

Cabbage Rolls With Peanut Sauce

Artist Maggie Wilder, whose painting decorates this section, makes good use of the Valley's fresh produce with this savory dish.

SERVES 4.

1 onion or 1 bunch green onions, chopped

1 1/2 cups mushrooms, sliced

1/2 cup mung bean sprouts

1/2 cup almonds, chopped

1 tablespoon olive oil

1 tablespoon soy sauce

Salt and pepper to taste

2 cups cooked brown rice

1 head Savoy cabbage

PREHEAT oven to 350°.

SAUTÉ onion, mushrooms, sprouts, and almonds in oil until onions are transparent, then add seasonings.

IN MIXING BOWL combine sautéed mixture with cooked rice and set aside while making sauce.

SAUCE:

1 cup vegetable or chicken broth

3 tablespoons chunky peanut butter

3 tablespoons soy sauce

4 tablespoons cornstarch

1/2 cup cold water

Cayenne to taste

IN A SAUCEPAN, heat broth, peanut butter, and soy sauce to boiling.

WHISK cornstarch into water until smooth. Add to boiling mixture slowly, whisking constantly until mixture is clear and smooth. Add cayenne.

STIR 1/2 cup of sauce into sautéed vegetable mixture.

SEPARATE leaves from cabbage head.

PLACE 1/2 to 3/4 cup of vegetable rice mixture in center of cabbage leaf and roll up. Repeat until all filling mixture is used.

PLACE filled rolls in flat baking dish. Pour remaining sauce over top and bake for 30 minutes.

Winter Fields, Fir Island, Clayton James

PASTAS, GRAINS, SAUCES

Two Roads On The Same Day

I. Flats
no thing in mind
but maverick daffodils
in the rye

through rain
the fields saw
themselves

grow over
the Norwegian farmhouse
on the flats

II. Poplars
fractious, words bark at the night
disavow connection

the Van Gogh poplars
receive wet homage

silent, in the rain
an aria, an opera, a seed.

—Peter Heffelfinger

Gorgonzola & Olive Oil Pasta

Joe Lamantia is known throughout western Washington for his Skagit River Bakery breads, produced in an ancient brick oven at his historic Mount Vernon bakery. He also creates flavorful pasta sauces, such as Gorgonzola and Olive Oil Pasta, and Marinara Sauce.

SERVES 4.

6 cloves garlic, whole

1 cup olive oil

1 bunch basil, torn

1 cup walnuts, chopped

1/2 pound mushrooms, sliced

2 teaspoons red hot peppers, minced

1 tablespoon balsamic vinegar

1 1-pound package linguini

1 pound Gorgonzola cheese, crumbled

Fresh-grated parmesan cheese

SAUTÉ garlic in olive oil.

ADD basil, walnuts, mushrooms, peppers, and vinegar, and sauté for 1/2 hour, stirring occasionally.

COOK linguini and toss with sautéed mixture.

SPRINKLE cheeses over pasta and serve immediately.

Bacon Fettucine

SERVES 6 TO 8.

1/2 pound lean bacon, cut into 1-inch pieces

5 tablespoons lemon juice

2 teaspoons crushed garlic, divided in half

2 small zucchini, chopped

1 medium onion, chopped

8 ounces mushrooms, sliced

1 bunch fresh spinach, cleaned, stemmed, patted dry, and chopped

4 tablespoons butter

1/3 cup dry white wine

1 pint whipping cream

1 tablespoon Dijon mustard

1/4 cup fresh grated parmesan cheese, for topping

1 cup fresh tomatoes, chopped for topping

1 pound fettucine, cooked and drained

OPTIONAL ADDITIONS:

1 jar marinated artichokes, drained and chopped

1 cup cooked chicken breast, skinned and chopped

PLACE bacon pieces in large non-reactive skillet and cook until well done.

DRAIN off all but 1 tablespoon of bacon fat and return skillet to burner.

TURN heat to medium high. Add lemon juice and 1 teaspoon garlic, then add the zucchini and onions and cook for 2 minutes.

ADD mushrooms; cook 2 minutes more.

ADD butter, rest of garlic, wine, and spinach. (If using artichokes and/or chicken, add them at this point.)

TURN heat up to high and add whipping cream and mustard to sauce. Cook until cream thickens, stirring to prevent sticking.

REMOVE sauce from heat and toss with cooked fettucine to coat well.

TURN into serving dish and top with cheese and tomatoes.

Garlic Pasta With Triple-Crème Cheese

Simplicity plus, this rich and creamy pasta recipe by artist Ed Kamuda is one of his favorites. He refers to it as "joy food."

SERVES 2.

2-inch wedge St. Andre's Triple-Crème cheese, 1/4 to 1/3 pound

2 quarts water

1/2 teaspoon salt

8-ounce package of fresh garlic pasta

GARNISH:

Chopped parsley and/or chives

BRING water and salt to a boil in large pot and add pasta.

WHILE PASTA COOKS, fill a serving bowl with boiling water to heat the bowl.

WHEN PASTA is almost done, dump water out of serving bowl. Add cheese, broken up with a fork.

DRAIN pasta and place over cheese. Toss well to melt cheese and garnish.

NOTE: Ed orders St. Andre's Triple-Crème cheese through local caterer Georgia Johnson. I found it at Larry's Market in Seattle.

Chilled Lemon Noodles With Mustard Shrimp

A recipe from Linda Patterson who called me one day and said, "Lavone, I know you have had a rough week, let's hike to the top of Big Rock." When we arrived at the summit, she unloaded her backpack and proceeded to wine and dine me with Lemon Noodles and Mustard Shrimp, *Chardonnay in pewter wine glasses, and fresh straw-berries to dip in* Gingered Vanilla Yogurt *(page 185).*

SERVES 4.

4 quarts of water

6 ounces dry, thin noodles or vermicelli

IN LARGE POT, bring water to a boil.

ADD noodles and cook uncovered, stir-ring occasionally, until tender, about 10 minutes.

DRAIN and rinse with cold water for about 2 minutes until noodles are cool and drain again.

TOSS with lemon dressing and mustard shrimp *(see below).*

LEMON DRESSING:

1/4 cup freshly-squeezed lemon juice

2 tablespoons soy sauce

2 teaspoons fresh ginger, finely chopped

2 teaspoons sesame oil

1 teaspoon sugar

COMBINE all ingredients and stir well.

POUR over cooled noodles and chill.

MUSTARD SHRIMP:

1/4 cup butter or olive oil

4 cloves garlic, minced or pressed

1/2 cup onion, finely chopped

1/4 teaspoon cayenne

1 1/2 pounds large raw shrimp, shelled and deveined

1/2 cup dry sherry

1/2 cup white wine vinegar

2 tablespoons Dijon mustard

2 tablespoons fresh tarragon, finely chopped

MELT butter or heat oil in frying pan over medium heat.

ADD garlic, onion, and cayenne. Sauté until onion is golden, about 5 minutes, stirring constantly.

ADD shrimp and continue to stir while cooking until the shrimp (cut to test) are opaque in center, about 4 or 5 minutes.

ADD sherry, vinegar, mustard, and tar-ragon. Stir until it boils. Cool.

COVER and chill for at least an hour or overnight before serving.

Seashell Pasta Bake

This dish can be made up to 2 days in advance. If frozen, thaw completely before baking.

SERVES 8 TO 10.

1 1-pound package large seashell pasta

1 10-ounce package frozen chopped spinach

1 pound ricotta cheese

1/2 pound mozzarella cheese, grated

1 cup fresh-grated parmesan cheese

1 tablespoon dried basil

4 ounces smoked ham or prosciutto, diced

4 cups prepared marinara sauce

PREHEAT oven to 350°.

COOK the pasta according to package directions, drain, and set aside.

MIX remaining ingredients together well, except sauce.

FILL each shell about half-full of mixture and press to seal.

POUR 1 cup of sauce into a 9x13-inch baking pan.

ARRANGE shells, seam side up on sauce. Pour remaining sauce over the top and cover with foil.

BAKE pasta for 30 minutes, remove foil, and serve immediately.

Asian-Inspired Steamed Grains & Rices

SERVES 5 TO 6.

1/4 cup brown lentils

1/4 cup basmati rice

1/4 cup wild rice

1/4 cup brown rice

2 tablespoons extra-virgin olive oil

1 1/2 cups water, boiling

IN A SKILLET, over medium to high heat, sauté lentils and rice for approximately 5 minutes in olive oil, stirring constantly with wooden spoon.

ADD boiling water, cover, reduce heat to lowest setting, and simmer for approximately 10 minutes. Turn heat off without removing lid, and let sit for 10 to 15 minutes. *(It is important not to remove lid for entire cooking process.)*

Basic Brown Rice

These directions for making brown rice are from Beverly Swanson, Nutrition Educator for a popular shopping destination in Mount Vernon—the Skagit Valley Food Co-op.

SERVES 4 TO 6.

2 cups water

1 cup brown rice or 3/4 brown and 1/4 wild rice

1/4 teaspoon sea salt

1 tablespoon oil

USE 2 to 1 ratio of water to rice. For lighter, fluffier results, use long grain variety. For stickier consistency, use short grain. You may substitute 1/4 cup wild rice for 1/4 cup brown rice to create a wonderful nutty flavor.

RINSE rice in colander under cold water.

IN MEDIUM SAUCEPAN, add salt and oil to water. Bring to rapid boil and add rice.

REDUCE heat to low, cover, and simmer for 45 to 50 minutes. Do not remove lid while cooking.

PILAF VARIATION:
SUBSTITUTE chicken broth for water.

SEASON at end of cooking with fresh herbs of choice, 1 tablespoon finely grated lemon, and garlic pepper. Add butter if desired.

Thai Peanut Sauce

Rick Carlson's piquant, fragrant sauce brings a taste of the Orient to Skagit Valley.

MAKES APPROXIMATELY 3 CUPS SAUCE.

2 13.5-ounce cans coconut milk*

1-2 tablespoons curry paste*

1-2 tablespoons nam prik paw (roasted chili in oil) *(See recipe below.)*

1/4 cup raw sugar

1 cup crunchy peanut butter

3 tablespoons tamarind juice*

1 teaspoon Chinese Five Spice*

1 teaspoon salt

* Available in Asian food section of super-markets.

IN A SAUCEPAN, stir-fry the curry paste, nam prik paw, and cream from top of coconut milk for 5 minutes.

ADD peanut butter, raw sugar, and tamarind juice.

SERVE over roasted or stir-fried meats and/or steamed vegetables; spread on toast, or use as a cold dip.

Chili In Oil (Nam Prik Paw)

MAKES APPROXIMATELY 1 1/2 CUPS.

1/2 cup dried hot red chilies

1/2 cup onion, green onion, or shallot, chopped

1/2 cup garlic, peeled

1/2 cup canola oil

1/4 cup raw sugar

ROAST chilies in an ungreased pan over low heat until brown. Remove from heat.

WHEN COOL, stem, and mince. For a more mild dish, discard seeds.

ROAST onion and garlic in the same pan until wilted, stirring to prevent burning.

GRIND chilies, onion, and garlic together in mortar or food processor.

FRY this paste in oil for 5 minutes over medium heat.

STIR in raw sugar. Cool, transfer to jar and seal tightly. Store in refrigerator.

Herb Butter

Ann Childs describes the following as "just swell to spread on French bread and heat up for a feast. It's green, pungent and piquant."

MAKES APPROXIMATELY 1 1/2 CUPS.

Juice of 1/2 lemon
1/2 cup melted butter or margarine
1 garlic clove
Fresh ground pepper, to taste
At least 1 cup fresh herbs*

*NOTE: Use bunch of chives. Try oregano or basil. Lemon balm and fennel are milder options.

GREEK STYLE:
Add 1 Tablespoon feta cheese with oregano and parsley as fresh herbs.

PESTO CLONE:
Add a little parmesan cheese with basil as fresh herb.

ARAB:
Use oregano and mint as fresh herbs. (A few grapes, or a touch of orange juice, add mystery.)

PURÉE all ingredients in blender.

Grenoblaise Butter

A savory sauce to use on fish and shellfish. It is also delicious on sautéed veal.

MAKES APPROXIMATELY 1 CUP.

1/2 pound sweet butter
Pulp and juice of 1 lemon
1 tablespoon capers, rinsed
3 tablespoons parsley, chopped
Salt and pepper to taste

HEAT butter until deep brown (but not burned). Cool.

SCRAPE butter into mixing bowl. Add other ingredients and whip until fluffy and white. You may freeze this butter in small balls for use later.

Marinara Sauce

SERVES 6 TO 8.

12 cloves garlic, minced or sliced

1/2 cup olive oil

1 medium red onion puréed in food processor

1 bunch fresh basil, chopped

2 teaspoons red hot peppers, chopped

3 large sprigs fresh oregano or 2 tablespoons dried

2 tablespoons balsamic vinegar

4 16-ounce cans diced tomatoes

1 quart chicken broth (homemade or canned)

SAUTÉ garlic in oil until golden.

ADD onion, basil, peppers, and oregano and sauté together for 1/2 hour.

ADD vinegar, tomatoes, and chicken broth. Bring all to a boil and turn heat down so sauce just simmers.

SIMMER about 3 hours. Meat or tofu can be added during simmering process.

SERVE over your favorite pasta.

Ann's Sweet Curry

Ann Childs likes to make her own curry powder. This is my favorite of three versions. It is very good in Helen Roozen's Haché *(page 87).*

MAKES APPROXIMATELY 1/2 CUP CURRY POWDER.

3 teaspoons cumin seed

3 teaspoons whole cloves

3 teaspoons cardamon seed

3 teaspoons seeds of dried cayenne or other very hot peppers

1 1/2 teaspoons anise or fennel seed

ROAST seeds in a pan on low to medium burner until seeds start to brown. (If they begin to pop like popcorn, remove from heat.) Stir occasionally with a wooden spoon as they brown. Or brown seeds for about 90 seconds in microwave.

REMOVE from heat and grind (Ann has an old coffee grinder she uses just for grinding seeds). Be aware that the fumes are strong. Do not put your face near the grinder when removing the lid.

COMBINE GROUND SEEDS WITH:

2 teaspoons cinnamon powder

2 teaspoons ginger powder

2 teaspoons fresh-grated nutmeg

2 teaspoons turmeric powder

WHEN ALL SPICES are combined, store in an airtight container.

NOTE: You can save time by omitting the roasting and grinding process and blending 2 teaspoons each of powdered cumin, cloves, cardamon, cayenne, and 1 teaspoon of powdered anise or fennel. The curry powder will be less intense but still very good.

Rhubarb-Mango Chutney

This chutney compliments Citrus Cilantro Chicken *(page 73).*

MAKES APPROXIMATELY 5 CUPS.

3 cups fresh rhubarb, thinly sliced

1 large ripe mango, peeled and chopped

4 green onions, chopped

1/2 cup raspberry vinegar

1 1/2 tablespoons fresh ginger, grated

1/8 teaspoon cayenne

3/4 cup dark brown sugar

1/3 cup blanched almonds, chopped

1 cup raisins

COMBINE first four ingredients in sauce-pan.

BRING TO A BOIL and simmer on low heat for 15 minutes.

ADD ginger, cayenne, sugar, and nuts and simmer for 15 more minutes.

ADD raisins and continue simmering until chutney has jam-like consistency, about 25 minutes.

SERVE warm or cold with steamed brown or white rice.

Lemon Mousse for Ham or Turkey

This tart Christmas buffet mousse was prepared for us by Annette Dold, a guest from Ebertsheim, Germany. It can also be served as a light dessert after a festive meal.

SERVES 10 TO 12.

3 lemons, both juice and grated rind

2 packages unflavored gelatin

3/4 cup whipping cream

1/2 cup sugar

1 cup plain unsweetened yogurt

Grate lemons and set rind aside.

Cut lemons in half and juice.

PLACE 1/2 cup of lemon juice in small saucepan, sprinkle with unflavored gelatin and let sit for 1 minute.

HEAT juice and gelatin over low heat, stirring until gelatin is completely dissolved. Remove from heat.

IN A MIXING BOWL, beat cream until stiff and add sugar.

IN A SECOND BOWL, combine gelatin, remaining lemon juice, and lemon peel with yogurt.

SLOWLY BLEND gelatin mixture into whipped cream mixture. *(I use an electric beater on slow speed)*

POUR mixture into gelatin mold and refrigerate until ready to serve.

UNMOLD on a plate by turning mold upside-down and placing a hot towel over it briefly.

Coffee Sauce

This is an adaptation of the coffee sauce served on pancakes (crepes) that 92-year-old Lyman resident Mary Albertine McDougle remembers her Austrian mother making for the family when Mary was a child. This sauce is good for dessert crepes, still widely eaten in Austria and increasingly popular here. (See recipe for Austrian Dessert Crepes *on page 173.)*

MAKES APPROXIMATELY 2 CUPS.

1/3 cup Italian or French-roast coffee beans, freshly ground

3/4 cup boiling water

1 tablespoon butter

1 1/2 tablespoons flour

1/2 cup milk

1 vanilla bean, sliced in half lengthwise

2 egg yolks, beaten

Pinch of salt

1/3 to 1/2 cup sugar

1/2 cup whipping cream

PLACE fresh-ground coffee in a filter over a cup and pour boiling water through.

MELT butter in a saucepan. Blend flour into butter and slowly whisk in milk. Whisk constantly over medium heat until sauce boils and becomes thick and smooth.

ADD vanilla bean halves.

STIR some of the hot mixture into beaten egg yolks, then whisk egg yolk mixture into hot sauce.

COOK on low heat for 2 minutes, stirring constantly.

REMOVE from heat and stir in coffee, salt, and sugar. Stir until sugar is dissolved. Chill.

WHEN SAUCE IS COOL, remove vanilla bean halves and fold in stiffly-beaten whipped cream. If not using immediately, refrigerate up to 2 days in tightly covered jar.

NOTE: This sauce is also delicious over chocolate ice cream or cake.

Rhubarb Berry Sauce for Fish or Lamb

A colorful sauce with a zing that is especially good with poached salmon or roasted lamb.

MAKES 2 TO 2 1/2 CUPS SAUCE.

2 cups rhubarb, chopped

2 tablespoons water

1/2 cup raw sugar or to taste

1 cup blueberries or blackberries

1 tablespoon creamed horseradish

GARNISH:

Mint leaves or edible flowers

COMBINE rhubarb and water in a saucepan and bring to a simmering boil.

COOK until rhubarb is tender, stirring occasionally to prevent sticking.

ADD sugar and continue to cook for another 10 to 15 minutes.

STIR in berries and horseradish. Simmer for at least 5 minutes to combine flavors.

DRIBBLE warm sauce over or under fish or lamb and garnish. Remaining sauce can be served in a gravy boat.

Quick Hot Applesauce

2 cups canned sweetened applesauce

1 tart fresh apple, peeled and chopped

1 tablespoon raw sugar

1/2 teaspoon grated lemon peel

HEAT canned applesauce to a boil in a medium saucepan.

ADD chopped apple and sugar to boiling sauce and simmer until chopped apple is tender but still retains its shape.

ADD lemon peel and remove from heat. Serve warm.

Exploding Potato, Philip McCracken

BREADS

GOD GRANT THE PRACTICAL SHAPE OUR DAYS

These things make us
day by day: colanders filled with new potatoes,
griddles and breadbowls, crockery smelling of brine,
the canning kettle, hoes and froes and scythes,
rasps, levels, drawknives, stones:
no room for trinkets.

The whack of a maul ends the day. Fire
tonight.

—JEAN MARIE HALLINGSTAD

Traditional Skillet Flatbread

Laura Wilbur, an elder of the Swinomish Indian Tribe, offers the following traditional Indian flatbread recipe. It is cooked in a heavy iron skillet over an open fire reduced to a bed of coals. When her boys were young, they began to disappear for a short time each day and would return home munching on a big hunk of hot skillet bread. They had made friends with a very old Indian couple who lived nearby in a tiny house on the banks of the Swinomish Channel. Every day Charley Blode and his wife cooked a skillet of flat bread over an outdoor fire. As soon as it was cooked, Charley would cut each of the boys a generous portion and they would head for home with their prize.

SERVES 4.

1 teaspoon salt

2 teaspoons baking powder

4 cups flour

Approximately 1 1/3 cups water

Butter for greasing pan

MIX salt and baking powder with flour in large bowl. Stir in enough cold water to form a fairly stiff dough.

SHAPE into flat round about 3/4-inch thick and place in heavily greased iron skillet. Set over a bed of hot coals.

WHEN BREAD IS GOLDEN brown on bottom (lift edge up to check with thin spatula), about 10 to 15 minutes, prop the skillet up on its side with a stick and with the uncooked portion facing the heat of the coals.*

WHEN NICELY BROWNED, remove from heat and serve hot.

*Some cooks prefer to use 2 tablespoons of butter to grease the skillet and flip the bread with a pancake turner instead of propping it up to brown the top.

Jamtland Bread

Joe and Anna Carlson arrived in Skagit Valley in 1926, settling east of Mount Vernon near Big Rock. Like many other immigrants of Swedish heritage, they joined the Vasa Lodge and Anna has several of her recipes in the Vasa Scandinavian Kitchens *cookbook. Jamtland is the Swedish state where Joe Carlson was born. It is traditional there to serve hard or soft flatbread as part of the Christmas Eve feast. Consequently, the recipe is meant to feed a large group.*

MAKES 20 TO 24 FLATBREADS.

3 packages dry yeast

3 cups lukewarm water

1 cup mashed potatoes

1 cup milk

1/2 cup brown sugar

1/2 cup dark corn syrup

1 tablespoon salt

2 teaspoons anise seed

1 cup rye flour

1/2 cup oil

Enough all-purpose flour to make a stiff dough, approximately 11 cups

DISSOLVE yeast in 1/2 cup lukewarm water.

COMBINE all ingredients, except yeast mixture and all-purpose flour, in large mixing bowl. Beat with electric mixer until well blended.

ADD yeast and continue to beat. Keep beating, adding flour two cups at a time, until too thick for the mixer. Use wooden spoon to complete mixing.

WHEN DOUGH comes away from sides of bowl, turn out onto floured board. Knead for about 5 minutes or until dough is smooth and elastic.

ROLL dough out very thin. Brown on both sides on a lightly greased griddle.

FOR SOFTER BREAD, place slightly damp, warm cloth over it briefly before serving.

NOTE: This bread freezes well. Remove from wrapping to thaw.

Anna's Hardanger Lefse

This is a traditional lefse from Anna Carlson, who makes it with a hand-carved, hand-made rolling pin, created by her dad for this purpose. The Carlson family likes to serve lefse warm, dripping with butter, wrapped around a piece of homemade potato sausage.

MAKES APPROXIMATELY 1 DOZEN LEFSE.

2 teaspoons baking soda

2 cups buttermilk

1/2 cup sugar

1/2 cup pineapple juice

1/2 cup light corn syrup

2 teaspoons salt

3 beaten eggs

Flour as needed, approximately 9 cups

ADD soda to buttermilk, combine with rest of ingredients, adding enough flour to make stiff dough that you can roll out very thin.

SHAPE dough into pieces the size of your lightly-oiled griddle. Brown lightly on each side.

NOTE: If you prefer a very soft lefse, briefly cover it with damp warm cloth before serving.

Southern Spoon Bread

One of my Lyman "Tarheel" neighbors from years ago introduced me to spoon bread. She insists that white cornmeal is better than yellow.

SERVES 6.

3 cups milk

3/4 cup white cornmeal

2 tablespoons butter

3/4 teaspoon salt

1 teaspoon baking powder

3 eggs, separated

1 17-ounce can or 2 cups fresh corn kernals

PREHEAT oven to 350°.

IN A MEDIUM SAUCEPAN, stir together 1 cup milk and cornmeal. Set aside.

IN A SECOND SAUCEPAN, scald the other 2 cups milk. Whisk into cornmeal mixture and cook over medium heat until thick.

REMOVE from heat and whisk in butter.

ADD salt and baking powder to egg yolks and beat well. Add this mixture to cornmeal and continue to beat until well blended.

BEAT egg whites until stiff. Fold into cornmeal and yolk mixture.

FOLD in corn (drain canned corn). Pour into greased casserole dish and bake for 1 hour.

SERVE cornbread with spoon. Especially good with fried fish.

Croatian Cornmeal Cheese Bread

During festivals in Anacortes, the Vela Luka Dance group often has a popular booth featuring traditional Croatian foods.

SERVES 6.

4 egg whites

4 egg yolks

1 1/2 cups quark cheese or dry cottage cheese

1/2 cup cheddar cheese, grated

1/4 teaspoon salt

2 tablespoons oil or melted butter

1 1/4 cups cornmeal

3/4 cup milk

PREHEAT oven to 350°.

BEAT egg whites in mixing bowl until they hold peaks. Set aside.

IN SECOND BOWL, beat egg yolks until thick and lemony.

ADD cheeses and beat until smooth.

BEAT in oil and salt.

ADD cornmeal alternately with milk, beating until smooth.

FOLD egg whites gently into batter until one color.

PREHEAT cast-iron skillet in oven for 5 minutes. Add oil or butter and swish around sides of skillet. Pour in batter.

BAKE cheese bread for 30 minutes or until golden. It is especially good served with Croatian Cabbage Rolls *(page 86)*.

Whole Wheat Bread

Laurie Olds, a member of the pioneer Good family, shared this recipe. Her grandmother Celia arrived on Fir Island from South Dakota with her mother in 1886. Laurie and her children Jeff and Kelsy are the fourth and fifth generation to live in the Good family home. Laurie remembers how she and the neighborhood kids could hardly wait to get off of the school bus and head to Grandma Celia's for freshly baked goodies.

MAKES 3 LOAVES.

4 cups boiling water

2 cups old-fashioned rolled oats

1/2 cup dark molasses

3 tablespoons cooking oil

1 teaspoon salt

2 tablespoons yeast

1 cup lukewarm water

5 cups whole wheat flour

6 to 7 cups unbleached flour

PREHEAT oven to 350°.

POUR boiling water over oats in large bowl.

ADD molasses, oil, and salt. Cool to luke-warm.

MEANWHILE, in another bowl, dissolve yeast in lukewarm water.

COMBINE the two mixtures and stir well.

ADD whole wheat flour, one cup at a time, blending thoroughly. Add un-bleached white flour and continue mixing until dough pulls away from sides of bowl.

TURN OUT onto floured board or countertop and knead until dough is smooth and elastic, from 5 to 10 minutes. Put finished dough in large, lightly greased bowl and cover with towel. Place in draft-free area for approximately 1 hour.

WHEN DOUGH HAS DOUBLED in bulk, punch down. Turn out onto board and knead briefly.

DIVIDE dough into three pieces and shape into loaves or rolls.

PLACE loaves into lightly greased bread pans and cover with towels. When dough has reached top of pan and springs back to the touch, it is ready to bake.

BAKE 30 minutes or until bread sounds hollow when tapped.

Grandma Newell's Swedish Limpa

Over the years I have collected many bread recipes. One of my favorites is Swedish limpa, an original recipe given to me by my late mother-in-law Viola Newell.

MAKES 3 LOAVES.

3 cups warm water

4 cakes fresh yeast or packages dry yeast

1/2 cup molasses

3/4 cup sugar

2 teaspoons salt

1 tablespoon fennel seed

1 tablespoon anise seed

Grated rind of 2 oranges

4 tablespoons of oil or butter

5 to 6 cups whole wheat flour, or un-
    bleached white flour (or half of each)

5 cups rye flour

PREHEAT oven to 350°.

DISSOLVE yeast in 1/2 cup of water and set aside.

COMBINE rest of water with molasses, sugar, salt, and seeds in saucepan. Bring to a boil and boil for one minute. Remove from heat and cool to lukewarm.

ADD yeast mixture, orange rind, oil, and flour.

KNEAD dough on floured surface until smooth and elastic, about 5 to 10 minutes. Place in greased bowl, cover, and let rise for two hours in warm room.

PUNCH down and let rise for another hour.

PUNCH down again and divide dough into three pieces. Form into three loaves. Place in greased bread pans and let rise an hour or until doubled. Bake 30 to 40 minutes or until bread sounds hollow when tapped.

Finnish Seed Rye Bread

MAKES 3 TO 4 LOAVES.

2 packages dry yeast

1/4 cup warm water

1 teaspoon sugar

4 cups buttermilk

1 egg or equivalent egg substitute

2 tablespoons honey

1 1/2 teaspoons salt

2 tablespoons fennel seed

2 tablespoons sesame seed

1/4 to 1/2 cup sunflower seeds

2 teaspoons crushed anise seed

2 tablespoons grated orange peel

1/2 cup canola oil

5 cups rye flour

8 cups, more or less, unbleached white flour

PREHEAT oven to 375°.

DISSOLVE yeast and sugar in warm water in large mixing bowl.

ADD buttermilk. Stir in egg, honey, salt, seeds, orange peel, and oil.

GRADUALLY BEAT in rye flour (the more you beat it, the less kneading you will need to do). Slowly beat in white flour, a little at a time. When dough becomes too stiff to use beater, stir in flour with wooden spoon until you find it difficult to stir.

TURN OUT dough onto floured board and knead in as much of remaining flour as it takes to make smooth, elastic dough. Place in a lightly greased large bowl, cover with cloth, and allow to rise in warm place until doubled in bulk, 1 to 2 hours.

PUNCH down. Turn out onto lightly oiled surface and divide into 3 or 4 pieces. Shape into round loaves.

SPRAY round cake pans or cookie sheet with baking spray. Place each loaf on prepared baking pans with smooth side up.

COVER and let rise until almost doubled, about an hour. Slash tops with sharp knife or razor blade in three parallel cuts across length and width of loaf, creating 1-inch squares.

BAKE for 40 to 45 minutes or until loaves sound hollow when tapped.

Multi-Grain Machine Bread

MAKES 1 MEDIUM LOAF.

3/4 cup cracked wheat

1/2 cup quinoa grain

1 1/2 tablespoons oil

2 tablespoons honey

1 egg

1 teaspoon salt

1 cup rolled 7-, 10-, or 12-grain cereal

1 1/4 cups whole wheat flour

1 3/4 cups all-purpose flour

3 tablespoons gluten flour

2 teaspoons yeast

SOAK grains in baking pan with 1 3/8 cup cold water for 30 minutes, then add remaining ingredients.

BAKE in bread machine on regular "white bread" cycle.

NOTE: Special flours can always be found in food co-ops.

Mrs. Durham's Pancakes

The recipe for these tender pancakes has been in the Peggy Enderlein family for several generations. Mrs. Durham was the Enderlein family cook.

MAKES APPROXIMATELY 16 PANCAKES.

Scant cup unsifted flour
1 teaspoon baking soda
1 teaspoon baking powder
2 tablespoons sugar
Pinch of salt
2 tablespoons oil
2 eggs
2 cups buttermilk

BEAT together all ingredients.

LADLE 1/4 cup or less batter onto lightly greased griddle and cook on medium heat until bubbles begin to pop.

TURN and cook until done.

SERVE pancakes with butter and heated syrup or place teaspoon of favorite jam on each pancake. Roll up and dust with powdered sugar.

Quick Ricotta Pancakes

These tender gourmet pancakes are based on a recipe that Shannon Good presented to her Skagit friends one Christmas.

MAKES 6 TO 8 PANCAKES.

2 eggs, beaten
1 cup low fat ricotta cheese
1 tablespoon honey
2 tablespoons melted butter or margarine
1/2 cup biscuit mix
1/4 teaspoon fresh-grated nutmeg

BLEND eggs and ricotta cheese in mixing bowl.

ADD honey and melted butter and beat in slowly.

BLEND in biscuit mix and nutmeg.

COOK on preheated griddle sprayed with butter-flavored cooking spray.

NOTE: Try these pancakes filled with chopped fresh fruit—fresh blueberries, sliced peaches, and bananas—stirred into nonfat yogurt. Place 1 heaping teaspoon on edge of each pancake, roll up, sprinkle with sifted powdered sugar, and serve with more yogurt.

Angel Biscuits

Angel biscuits are a traditional "Tarheel" bread. Irma Dills, a North Carolina native, brought this recipe with her when she moved to the Hamilton area of Skagit Valley many years ago.

MAKES 18 TO 24 BISCUITS.

5 cups unsifted flour

1/4 cup sugar

3 teaspoons baking powder

1 teaspoon soda

1 teaspoon salt

1 cup shortening

1 package dry yeast

2 tablespoons warm water

2 cups buttermilk

Melted butter for dipping

PREHEAT oven to 400°.

SIFT dry ingredients together into mixing bowl.

CUT in shortening until mixture resembles coarse meal.

DISSOLVE yeast in warm water and add with buttermilk to dry ingredients. Mix well and turn out on lightly floured surface. Roll dough out to scant 1/2-inch thickness. If too sticky, add a little more flour. Cut into rounds with biscuit cutter.

DIP each biscuit in melted butter and fold over (or, for less fat, omit dipping and put a dab of soft butter between the fold, pinch together and place on oiled baking sheet).

PLACE on greased cookie sheet and let stand for 1 1/2 hours. Bake 20 to 25 minutes or until lightly browned.

Swedish Pancakes

The rule for making Swedish pancakes is to use twice as much milk as flour. Serve these thin delicacies as breakfast pancakes or as dessert crepes, made by topping them with fresh berries or sliced fresh fruit and a generous layer of sweetened whipped cream.

MAKES APPROXIMATELY 16 PANCAKES.

1 1/4 cups flour

2 1/2 cups milk

3 eggs, beaten

Pinch of salt

2 teaspoons sugar

3 tablespoons butter, melted

WHISK flour and milk alternately into eggs. Add salt and sugar and whisk until blended.

JUST BEFORE COOKING, add melted butter. Pour 1/4 cup or less batter onto middle of hot lightly oiled skillet and turn the pan to spread batter evenly.

WHEN PANCAKE SETS, turn over gently with spatula.

Ruth Bond's Welsh Tichen [Tiesen] Flats

This is a recipe from one of my mother's old church cookbooks published in the 1940s. The "flats" are a lot like cake doughnuts but not as greasy. Serve warm with butter and fresh-brewed coffee.

MAKES 18 SQUARES.

1/2 cup shortening

1/4 cup sugar

1 egg, beaten

3/4 cup buttermilk or sour cream

3 cups flour

1 1/2 teaspoons baking powder

1/4 teaspoon baking soda

1 teaspoon salt

2 teaspoons nutmeg, fresh-grated

1 cup raisins or currants

CREAM shortening and sugar.

ADD egg, milk, and sifted dry ingredients and mix well to make thin dough much like doughnut dough. Stir in raisins.

ROLL OUT on lightly floured surface to about 3/8-inch thick. Cut into 2 1/2-inch squares.

COOK squares on oiled pancake griddle or in electric skillet at medium-low heat. More oil may need to be added when squares are turned.

Skagit Berry Oatmeal Muffins

Peter Goldfarb serves these muffins at his Fir Island White Swan Guest House.

MAKES 12 MUFFINS.

DRY INGREDIENTS:

1/2 cup oatmeal

1/2 cup oat bran

1 1/2 cups flour

1/3 cup sugar

1 teaspoon salt

1 tablespoon baking powder

PREHEAT oven to 400°.

COMBINE dry ingredients.

WET INGREDIENTS:

1 egg

3/4 cup milk

1/2 cup vegetable oil

1 cup mixed berries, such as blueberries, halved strawberries, raspberries, or blackberries.

MIX in wet ingredients. Gently stir in berries just until mixed.

SPOON batter into greased 12-muffin tin. Sprinkle batter with topping *(below)*.

BAKE muffins for about 20 minutes, or until inserted toothpick comes out dry.

TOPPING:

1/3 cup oatmeal

1/4 cup brown sugar

1 teaspoon cinnamon

MIX together.

Peter Goldfarb's Ginger-Peachy Pecan Muffins

MAKES 12 TO 18 MUFFINS.

1/2 cup butter or margarine

1 1/4 cups sugar

2 eggs

1 teaspoon vanilla

2 cups flour

1/2 teaspoon salt

2 teaspoons baking powder

2 teaspoons ground ginger

1/2 cup milk

1 1/2 cups fresh peaches, chopped, peeled, and drained

1/2 cup pecans, chopped

PREHEAT oven to 375°.

CREAM butter, sugar, and vanilla until light.

ADD eggs one at a time, beating well after each addition.

SIFT flour, salt, baking powder, and ginger together. Add to creamed mixture alternately with milk.

FOLD in peaches and pecans.

FILL greased 12 to18-muffin tins 3/4 full with batter. Sprinkle tops lightly with granulated sugar. Bake for about 25 minutes. Cool 20 minutes before removing from muffin tins.

Swedish Almond Rusks

The following is a traditional Swedish recipe from Florence Ekstrand's Scandinavian Home Cooking *collection.*

MAKES ABOUT 7 DOZEN RUSKS.

1 cup shortening

1 1/2 cups sugar

2 eggs

2 teaspoons almond extract

5 cups flour

1 teaspoon soda

1 teaspoon salt

1 cup nonfat sour cream

1 cup chopped almonds

PREHEAT oven to 350°.

CREAM shortening and sugar. Add beaten eggs. Blend in almond extract.

SIFT dry ingredients. Add to creamed mixture alternately with sour cream and almonds.

DIVIDE dough into six equal parts. Shape into 15-inch-long rolls.

PLACE 3 rolls on each of two ungreased large cookie sheets. Allow space to spread in baking. Bake 30 minutes.

REMOVE rolls from cookie sheets and cut diagonally into 3/4-inch slices. Place slices cut side down on cookie sheets, return to oven and toast 10 to 15 minutes until brown. Turn rusks and toast other side.

COOL rusks and store in tightly covered container.

Christmas Biscotti

1/2 cup butter

3/4 cup sugar

3 eggs

1/2 teaspoon vanilla

3 cups flour

3 teaspoons baking powder

1/2 teaspoon salt

2 tablespoons grated lemon peel

2 tablespoons grated orange peel

1 tablespoon anise seed

1 cup chopped almonds

1/2 cup dried cranberries

PREHEAT oven to 350°.

USING ELECTRIC BEATER, cream butter and sugar.

BEAT in eggs one at a time, beating well after each addition. Beat in vanilla.

SIFT TOGETHER dry ingredients and add slowly to butter mixture.

STIR in peels, anise seed, nuts, and cranberries. When well mixed, divide dough into 3 pieces and shape each one into a roll about 1 1/2 inches in diameter.

PLACE rolls on a large cookie sheet as far apart as possible. Flatten them slightly. Bake for 15 minutes.

REMOVE from oven and cut each roll into 3/4-inch slices. Return slices to cookie sheet with cut sides down.

RETURN to oven and bake 12 to 15 minutes longer. When cool, store in airtight container. Delicious for dunking or munching.

Mom's Apple Rolls

2 cups flour

1/2 cup sugar

1/2 teaspoon salt

4 teaspoons baking powder

1/2 cup shortening

3/4 cup milk

1/2 cup rolled oats

1/3 to 1/2 cup melted butter

4 cups thinly sliced apples

1/2 cup brown sugar

1 teaspoon cinnamon

PREHEAT oven to 350°.

SIFT flour, sugar, salt, and baking powder together. Add shortening and milk. Stir until mixture forms a dough.

PLACE rolled oats on a pastry cloth. Place dough on oats and roll out thin, as for cinnamon rolls.

SLATHER rolled-out dough with melted butter, cover with sliced apples, and sprinkle with cinnamon and sugar.

ROLL UP and cut into 1-inch slices.

ARRANGE slices on greased cookie sheet and bake for 15 to 20 minutes, or until golden brown.

Easy Overnight Sweet Rolls

The following recipe is just the thing for unexpected overnight guests. Mix it before going to bed and slip it in the cold oven. Next morning turn the oven on and wait. Your guests will think you got up at the crack of dawn to prepare such a festive treat. Long-time Valley resident Maureen Johnson, of Big Lake, likes to make this recipe when she and husband Gene are out camping in their travel trailer.

MAKES 16 ROLLS.

1 6-ounce jar maraschino cherries, drained

1/2 cup chopped nuts of your choice

16 frozen bread rolls

1/2 cup brown sugar

1 package regular vanilla pudding mix

1/4 pound melted butter

GREASE bundt or tube pan and cover bottom with cherries and nuts.

ARRANGE rolls over cherry-nut mixture around ring.

MIX brown sugar and dry pudding mix and pour over rolls. Pour on melted butter. Cover with wet paper towel and place in cold oven overnight.

NEXT MORNING remove paper towel. Set oven at 350° and bake rolls for 30 minutes or until they sound hollow when tapped.

Nonfat Banana Bread

MAKES 1 LOAF.

1 cup flour

2/3 cup sugar

2 teaspoons baking powder

1/2 teaspoon salt

1 teaspoon apple pie spice*

1 cup mashed bananas

1/4 cup nonfat milk

2 eggbeaters (equivalent to 2 eggs)

1/4 cup nonfat banana yogurt, drained
   overnight

1 teaspoon vanilla

3/4 to 1 cup all-purpose flour

*To make your own apple pie spice, combine 1/2 teaspoon cinnamon, 1/4 teaspoon cloves, and 1/4 teaspoon nutmeg.

PREHEAT oven to 350°.

PLACE yogurt in sieve or coffee filter with container underneath and let drain in refrigerator overnight.

IN LARGE BOWL, mix first 5 ingredients.

ADD bananas, prepared yogurt, and milk. Beat with electric mixer at low speed until blended, then at high speed for 2 minutes.

ADD egg beaters, vanilla, and remaining flour. Beat until well blended.

POUR batter into loaf pan coated with nonfat cooking spray. Bake for approximately 1 hour or until toothpick comes out clean.

Nonfat Zucchini & Lime Bread

Chantelle Hilsinger, my oldest granddaughter, really searches for low-fat recipes. This is one of her favorites.

MAKES 1 LOAF.

2 cups flour

1 teaspoon ground cinnamon

1/2 teaspoon baking soda

1/4 teaspoon salt

1/4 teaspoon nutmeg

3/4 cup sugar

1/4 cup brown sugar

1 1/4 cup unpeeled zucchini, grated

1/4 cup nonfat milk

1 egg beater (equivalent to 1 egg)

1/2 teaspoon lime juice, freshly squeezed

1 teaspoon grated lime rind

PREHEAT oven to 350°.

IN A MIXING BOWL, combine dry ingredients.

IN ANOTHER BOWL, add remaining ingredients. Mix well.

ADD first mixture to second mixture. Mix until just blended, adding more flour as needed to keep batter from being runny.

POUR batter into loaf pan coated with nonfat cooking spray. Bake for approximately 1 hour or until toothpick comes out clean. Cool and wrap in plastic. Store overnight before slicing.

Wonderful Buttermilk Scones

In years past, I opened my home and studios to a group of Seattle's Lakeside High School students and teachers. While camping out here, they did art projects. Lakeside Library's glowing stained glass window is the product of one of these visits. Marcia Fischer attended workshops here in the early 1980s and has continued to visit periodically. She shared the following scone recipe. It is Marcia's adaptation of a Sarah Tousley recipe in the Lakeside Mothers' Cookbook.

MAKES 12 SCONES.

3 cups flour

1/4 cup sugar

2 1/2 teaspoons baking powder

1/2 teaspoon baking soda

1/2 teaspoon salt

3/4 cup butter

1 cup currants

Grated peel of one orange

1 cup buttermilk

PREHEAT oven to 425°.

COMBINE the first 5 ingredients in a mixing bowl; cut in butter until the mixture is in pea-sized grains.

ADD currants and orange peel. Make a well in the center and pour in buttermilk. Stir with a fork until dough leaves the sides of the bowl.

KNEAD dough briefly on a floured board.

DIVIDE dough into 3 balls. Flatten each with the palm of your hand until 1/2 to 3/4-inch thick. Shape into a circle and cut into quarters.

PLACE 12 quarter-pieces on ungreased cookie sheet. Bake for approximately 12 minutes or until golden. The scones freeze well.

Seeded Wheat Bread Machine Loaf

A high-protein, high-fiber bread that is a powerhouse of nutrition and flavor.

MAKES A 1 1/2 POUND LOAF.

1 1/4 cups water

3 tablespoons safflower oil

3 tablespoons honey

1 cup whole wheat flour

2/3 cup bread flour

1/3 cup dark rye flour

1/3 cup gluten flour

3 tablespoons buckwheat flour

2 tablespoons oat-blend flour

2 tablespoons oat bran

2 tablespoons wheat germ

2 tablespoons yellow cornmeal

3 tablespoons rolled oats

1/3 cup sunflower seeds

1 tablespoon sesame seeds

1 tablespoon flax seed

1 teaspoon anise seed (optional)

2 teaspoons grated orange peel (optional)

1 teaspoon sea salt

1/4 cup nonfat dry milk

4 teaspoon dry yeast

FIT the kneading blade firmly on shaft in bread pan. Add liquid ingredients.

IN MIXING BOWL, combine carefully measured dry ingredients except for yeast (to be added last). Stir in orange peel and transfer flour mixture to bread pan.

MAKE small indent in dry ingredients and place yeast in it without mixing in liquids.

PLACE the pan inside the machine and close the lid.

PROGRAM the automatic bread maker for whole wheat mode.

AT END OF BAKING CYCLE, remove bread promptly from machine, taking care to use potholders, as oven surfaces will be hot. Invert bread pan onto a wire rack and shake several times to dislodge bread.

Triumph of the Egg, Guy Anderson

DESSERTS

HOUSE

My grandmother,
for the joy of hearing the floor creak with
the mysterious feeling of damp cellars,
walks

over the kitchen floor.
Down there
a spider sleeps, legs folded together
making a witch's hand.
Listen: such silence gathers,
you hear
the generous orange squared heart of a fir beam
releasing a trickle of powder,
little grains falling to fleck the pale white long legs of
 old potatoes
reaching for their youth.

—ROBERT SUND

Austrian Dessert Crepes

MAKES 8 CREPES.

2 eggs

Pinch of salt

1 1/2 teaspoons sugar

1 cup milk

2 tablespoons cognac

Scrapings of 1 inch of vanilla bean

1 tablespoon butter, melted

2/3 cups all-purpose flour

WHISK eggs well in bowl and add rest of ingredients. Continue to whisk until smooth. Set batter aside for one hour.

OIL a 7-inch crepe pan and heat over medium-high until a drop of water sizzles when dropped in pan.

POUR a little less than 1/4 cup of batter into pan, tilting and rotating pan so batter coats surface evenly.

COOK until slightly browned on underside. Turn. When second side is cooked but not brown, turn out of pan onto towel with browned side up.

PLACE equal amounts of apple filling *(below)* on each crepe and roll them up.

PLACE crepes in flat baking dish, sprinkle with powdered sugar, and place under broiler until sugar glazes top. Top with whipped cream.

APPLE FILLING:

4 tart apples, peeled, cored, and coarsely
    chopped

3 tablespoons butter

1 teaspoon vanilla

1/4 cup powdered sugar for glazing

MELT butter in non-reactive skillet.

ADD apples and cook gently, covered, until tender but still firm. Stir in vanilla.

RICOTTA CHEESE VARIATION:

1/4 cup low-fat cream cheese

2/3 cup low-fat ricotta cheese or quark

Pinch of salt

1 tablespoon sugar

1 teaspoon grated lemon peel

1 tablespoon butter

COMBINE ingredients, except butter.

PLACE 1 tablespoon of filling in center of browned side of crepe.

FOLD two opposite sides of crepe over filling, then overlap the other two sides, into a neat rectangular package. Repeat.

MELT butter in large skillet. Arrange folded crepes, seam side down, in skillet. Brown both sides over moderate heat.

Garnish with currant jelly or sour cream.

Skagit Wild Blackberry Chantilly

Himalayan wild blackberries are found throughout the Valley. Use these large blackberries for making blackberry vinegar, pies, jelly, and wine. The elusive little wild blackberries, called dewberries, that appear in logged-over areas are harder to find and pick. No other berry has their zesty flavor.

SERVES 6.

4 cups of fresh or thawed frozen Himalayan wild blackberries

1/2 cup sugar, or more if needed

1 1/2 cups fresh or frozen mountain blackberries (dewberries)

1/2 cup Chantilly liqueur

1/2 cup whipping cream, stiffly whipped

PURÉE Himalayan blackberries in food processor or blender.

STRAIN seed remnants from pureed berries through fine sieve.

COMBINE purée with sugar and whole dewberries.

FOLD in whipped cream laced with liqueur.

DIVIDE mixture among dessert dishes and garnish with a few reserved blackberries or edible flowers.

OPTIONS:

LAYER Dreyer's Low-Fat French Silk Chocolate ice cream with berry mixture and whipped cream laced with Grand Marnier. Serve in parfait glasses.

SERVE with Melting Moments Shortbread Cookies *(page 190)* for added taste treat.

SUBSTITUTE 4 cups fresh rhubarb sauce sweetened with raw sugar for blackberry purée. Layer with Swiss Almond ice cream.

Grandma Love's Gingerbread

Becky Love let me browse through her grandmother's recipe box. Stuffed with a lifetime of caring, it had everything in it from a "recipe for cough syrup for momma," to the following recipe labeled "gingerbread, 100 year-old recipe." Since that notation was probably made in the 1940s, it is more likely a 150 year-old recipe now.

MAKES APPROXIMATELY 24 TWO-INCH SQUARES.

1/2 cup sugar

1/2 cup butter and lard mixed

1 egg

1 cup molasses

2 1/2 cups flour, sifted

1 1/2 teaspoon baking soda

1 teaspoon cinnamon

1 teaspoon ginger

1/2 teaspoon cloves

1/2 teaspoon salt

1 cup boiling water

PREHEAT oven to 350°.

CREAM sugar and butter-lard mixture in mixing bowl.

BEAT in egg and molasses.

SIFT dry ingredients together and add to mixture. Beat well.

BEAT in boiling water until smooth.

POUR into greased 9x13-inch cake pan and bake for 40 to 45 minutes or until gingerbread springs back at touch.

SERVE gingerbread squares warm with whipped cream or vanilla ice cream. Instead of adding sugar to stiffly beaten whipped cream, try blending in 2 tablespoons of Grand Marnier or crème de cacao and 1/4 cup unsweetened cocoa.

Apple Cake

Grace Park of LaConner shared her recipe for this delectable dessert.

4 cups raw apples, peeled and cubed

2 eggs

1/2 cup oil

1 1/2 teaspoons vanilla extract

2 cups white sugar

1 1/2 teaspoons cinnamon

1 1/2 cups chopped dates or citron

2/3 cup walnuts, chopped

2 cups all purpose flour

1 1/2 teaspoons soda

1 teaspoon salt

PREHEAT oven to 350°.

PLACE cubed apples in bowl. Break eggs over them and mix well.

ADD oil, vanilla, sugar, cinnamon, dates, and walnuts and stir together.

SIFT flour, soda, and salt together and add to apple mixture.

MIX with wooden spoon until flour mixture is thoroughly blended into apple mixture.

POUR batter into greased 9x13 baking pan and bake for 45 minutes. Serve warm or cold with whipped cream laced with Grand Marnier *(below)*.

GRAND MARNIER WHIPPED CREAM:

1 cup whipping cream

2 tablespoons Grand Marnier

1 tablespoon powdered sugar or to taste

WHIP cream in bowl until stiff.

SLOWLY BEAT in Grand Marnier and powdered sugar until blended.

Poppyseed Candlelight Cake

Susan Hayton of Fir Island gave me this recipe in the 1970s. It's an easy, quick version of poppyseed cake that will make people think you have been slaving in the kitchen all afternoon.

MAKES 1 ANGEL FOOD-SIZED CAKE.

1 package yellow or lemon cake mix

1 small package instant vanilla pudding

4 eggs

1 cup sour cream

1/2 cup salad oil

1/2 cup cream sherry

1/4 cup poppy seeds

PREHEAT oven to 350°.

COMBINE all ingredients in large mixing bowl and beat at medium speed for 2 minutes.

POUR into greased 10-inch bundt pan or angel-food cake pan.

BAKE for 45-50 minutes or until inserted toothpick comes out clean.

COOL cake in pan for 15 minutes. Invert and remove from pan and finish cooling on rack.

SPOON Orange Butter Glaze *(below)* over cooled cake.

DECORATE cake top and sides with edible flowers, such as blue borage, before glaze is set.

ORANGE BUTTER GLAZE:

1 1/2 tablespoons milk

1 tablespoon butter

1 tablespoon orange juice

1 1/2 cups powdered sugar

1 teaspoon grated orange peel

Edible flowers for decoration

IN A SMALL SAUCEPAN, combine milk, butter, and orange juice and stir over medium heat until butter is melted. Or combine ingredients in ceramic mixing bowl and microwave.

ADD powdered sugar and grated orange peel and beat until smooth.

Danish Potato Flour Torte

Mac MacGregor's mother's file is packed with wonderful recipes she collected over many years. Many recipes are accompanied by notes written back and forth between family members comparing the history and quality of particular recipes.

SERVES 12 TO 16.

4 large eggs, yolks and whites separated

1 cup sugar

1/2 teaspoon vanilla

1/2 cup potato flour

1 teaspoon baking powder

1/2 teaspoon salt

PREHEAT oven to 350°.

IN A BOWL, beat egg yolks until thick and fluffy. Gradually beat in 1/2 cup sugar and vanilla.

SIFT potato flour, baking powder, and salt together. Add to yolk-sugar mixture and beat well.

BEAT egg whites in separate bowl until they hold their shape. Gradually beat in remaining 1/2 cup sugar.

FOLD meringue into egg yolk mixture and pour batter into spring form torte pan, coated with butter-flavored cooking spray. Bake for 30 minutes. The torte will puff up during baking but will settle when cooling.

TOPPING:

1 cup heavy whipping cream

1/4 cup unsweetened cocoa

1/3 cup sugar

2 bananas, sliced

WHIP cream until stiff and beat in unsweetened cocoa and sugar.

LET STAND in refrigerator for 1 hour.

SPREAD chocolate cream over top of cooled cake.

ARRANGE sliced bananas over top and serve. (You may prefer to substitute 1/4 cup créme de cacao or Kahlua for sugar.)

Mom's Cheesecake

A family favorite from Linda Patterson, manager of Skagit County Treasurer's office and Big Lake resident.

SERVES 8 TO 10.

CRUST:

1 cup flour

1/4 cup sugar

1/2 cup butter

1 egg yolk, slightly beaten

1/4 teaspoon vanilla extract

PREHEAT oven to 400°.

COMBINE flour and sugar. Cut in butter until mixture is crumbly.

ADD egg yolk and vanilla. Blend well.

PAT 1/3 of dough on bottom of spring form pan, sides removed, and bake about 6 minutes until golden brown. Cool.

CHEESE FILLING:

3 8-ounce packages cream cheese

1 3/4 cups sugar

3 tablespoons flour

1/4 teaspoon salt

1/4 teaspoon vanilla extract

5 eggs (1 cup)

2 egg yolks

1/4 cup heavy cream

PREHEAT oven to 500°.

STIR softened cream cheese and then beat until fluffy.

COMBINE the next 4 ingredients and gradually blend them into cheese.

BEAT in eggs and yolks, one at a time, beating well after each is added. Gently stir in cream.

BUTTER sides of torte pan, attach to bottom. Pat remaining dough evenly on sides to a height of 2 inches.

POUR in cheese filling and bake for 5 to 8 minutes, or until top is golden brown.

TURN oven down to 200° and bake for 1 hour or until filling is set.

COOL 3 hours before removing sides of pan and glazing cake.

STRAWBERRY GLAZE TOPPING:

1 cup water

1 1/2 tablespoons corn starch

1/2 to 3/4 cup sugar

2 to 3 cups fresh strawberries, sliced

1 cup unsweetened canned pineapple, drained

COOK water, corn starch, and sugar in saucepan until clear and thick.

COOL and add fruit. Spoon over top of cheesecake.

Black Russian Cake

This recipe is sinful! It is a chocoholic's dream from Kathi Babraitis's collection of fabulous recipes. It is so simple and so decadent that I make it for every special occasion that comes along.

MAKES 1 BUNDT CAKE.

1 package devil's food cake mix

1 4-ounce package instant chocolate pudding mix

4 eggs

3/4 cup strong coffee, cold

3/4 cup coffee liqueur

3/4 cup créme de cacao

1/2 cup oil

PREHEAT oven to 350°.

GREASE and lightly flour a 10-inch bundt pan.

USING ELECTRIC MIXER, blend all cake ingredients in mixing bowl until batter forms.

POUR into bundt pan and bake 45 minutes or until tester inserted in center comes out clean.

LET COOL 10 minutes before removing from pan.

GLAZE:

1 cup powdered sugar

2 tablespoons strong coffee, cold

2 tablespoons coffee liqueur

2 tablespoons crème de cacao

IN SMALL BOWL, combine all glaze ingredients and stir until smooth.

INVERT warm cake onto rack over wax paper.

PIERCE top surface of cake with fork. Spoon glaze over and cool completely. Dust cake with additional powdered sugar before serving.

NOTE: Can be made up to 3 days ahead. Store in airtight container.

Fruit Pizza

The following recipe was given to me by Jo Ann Welling. It is elegant, belying its name. While visiting friends in Sweden, I volunteered to make it for a festive occasion. I made enough to serve 45 people. They loved it. It is flexible, in that you can use any fresh fruit available. In Sweden I used a basic sugar cookie recipe but it is much faster to use a package of Pillsbury sugar cookie dough from the refrigerated section of your supermarket. If you prefer to make your own, use the sugar cookie recipe on page 192.

SERVES 20.

1 package sugar cookie refrigerated mix or sugar cookie recipe from scratch.

8 ounces cream cheese, softened

4 ounces Kool Whip

1 20-ounce can crushed pineapple, well drained

PREHEAT oven to 350°.

PRESS dough evenly over bottom of 11x15-inch jelly roll pan.

BAKE until lightly browned, about 12 minutes. Cool.

LIGHTLY BEAT CREAM cheese and fold in Kool Whip. Spread over cooled cookie base.

SPREAD pineapple evenly over cream cheese mixture.

ARRANGE in patterns over pineapple any or all of the following:

> Fresh strawberries, sliced
> Fresh raspberries
> Fresh blueberries
> Banana slices
> Fresh peaches or nectarines, sliced
> Kiwis, peeled and sliced

DRIBBLE over the entire fruit-covered surface pre-cooked and cooled orange glaze *(recipe below)*. Cut pizza into 3-inch squares. If not serving immediately, refrigerate.

ORANGE GLAZE:

1 cup sugar

2 tablespoons cornstarch

1 cup frozen orange juice concentrate, undiluted

4 tablespoons lemon juice

BLEND ingredients in small saucepan and bring to a boil. Turn heat down and cook until thickened slightly and clear. Cool and pour over fruit on cookie base. Refrigerate until served.

Graham Cracker Apple Crisp

The following recipe was gleaned from a 1950 Concrete-area women's club recipe booklet titled The K.Y.N.C. Cooks. *Glancing through the names of the contributors created a time warp for me. Suddenly I was a teenager again, and all of those South Skagit women, including my mother, were in the room with me laughing, teasing, and enjoying each other's special foods. Sally Gross contributed this apple crisp to the booklet.*

SERVES 12.

1/4 cup butter

1/2 cup dark brown sugar

1 teaspoon cinnamon

1/2 teaspoon grated nutmeg

1 1/4 cups graham cracker crumbs

6 to 7 large tart apples

1/2 cup white sugar

PREHEAT oven to 350°.

HEAVILY BUTTER 9x13-inch baking dish.

CREAM butter, brown sugar, spices, and graham cracker crumbs together.

PEEL, core, and slice apples.

PLACE layer of sliced apples in buttered pan, sprinkle with half of white sugar (1/4 cup) and crumb mixture (5/8 cup).

REPEAT the layers, ending with crumb mixture. For a crunchy topping, dot with a little butter.

BAKE until apples are tender, about 40 minutes. Serve Apple Crisp warm or cold. French vanilla ice cream is a nice accompaniment.

Rhubarb Delight

Jan Johnson, who grows a variety of flowers for dry and fresh-cut bouquets at Larkspur Farm on Fir Island, brought this recipe to a potluck. It speaks of spring and luscious cooking.

SERVES 12.

2 cups sifted flour

1/3 cup powdered sugar

1 cup butter (2 sticks), cubed

4 eggs, beaten

2 1/2 cups sugar

1/2 cup flour

4 cups fresh spring rhubarb, chopped

PREHEAT oven to 350°.

MIX flour, powdered sugar, and butter to coarse meal consistency with pastry blender.

PRESS into 9x13-inch baking pan.

BAKE 15 minutes, or until light golden.

MIX remaining ingredients well and pour over baked crust.

RETURN to oven and bake 50 minutes or more, until rhubarb is tender. Cut into 12 squares and serve each with a scoop of ice cream.

Strawberry Shortcake, Kansas Style

Every fifth year my sister, June Stone, arrives home on leave from Central African Republic, where she has been a medical missionary for 35 years. This is her first food request. She even eats it for breakfast!

SERVES 8.

2 baked, flaky pie crusts

1/2 cup sugar

1 quart fresh strawberries, crushed

1/4 cup sugar or more

1 1/2 quarts fresh strawberries, thick sliced

1 pint whipping cream

2 tablespoons powdered sugar

1 teaspoon vanilla extract

Whole strawberries for garnish

STIR 1/2 cup sugar into crushed strawberries and set aside for a few minutes to let berries absorb sugar.

SPRINKLE 1/4 cup sugar over sliced strawberries and stir gently. Let sit for a few minutes so sugar is absorbed.

WHIP cream until stiff. Fold in the powdered sugar and vanilla extract.

TO ASSEMBLE:

JUST BEFORE SERVING, place one baked pie shell on large rimmed platter or serving dish.

LINE SHELL with 1/2 sliced strawberries. Cover with whipped cream and pour crushed strawberries over top.

PLACE second pie shell on top and repeat layers of berries and whipped cream.

CUT shortcake carefully into 8 portions and serve in dessert bowls, topping with reserved whole strawberries.

Fresh Strawberry Treats

Here are three different ways to serve the Valley's delicious fresh strawberries.

COAT fresh strawberries with sour cream. Arrange in dish and sprinkle with brown sugar.

OR, PLACE BOWL of fresh strawberries, with stems attached, next to bowl of sour cream, and second bowl of brown sugar, for dipping.

Strawberries With Gingered Vanilla Yogurt

1 1/2 cups vanilla yogurt

1/2 teaspoon powdered ginger

1 quart fresh strawberries, with stems

STIR yogurt and ginger together in bowl and arrange on tray with fresh strawberries with stems still attached. Ginger yogurt also makes a great fruit salad dressing.

Chocolate-Dipped Strawberries

1 12-ounce package of semi-sweet or milk chocolate chips

1/4 cup vegetable shortening

1 to 1 1/2 quarts fresh strawberries with stems

PLACE chips and shortening in top of double boiler over hot (not boiling) water and stir until mixture is melted and smooth.

REMOVE pan from heat but keep chocolate above hot water.

DIP whole fresh strawberries or other fresh fruit in chocolate. Shake off excess and place berries on wax paper or foil to set the chocolate. If chocolate begins to set while dipping, return to heat until melted again.

CHILL for 15 minutes before serving.

Amaretto Truffles

Georgia Johnson, a local caterer and owner of Georgia's Bakery in LaConner, made these irresistible white chocolate truffles for a gallery art opening.

MAKES ABOUT 1 1/2 POUNDS.

10 ounces high-quality white chocolate

2/3 cup heavy cream, scalded

1 teaspoon almond extract

1 teaspoon Amaretto liqueur

2 cups almond praline, finely chopped
    (see below)

MELT chocolate over hot water on low heat.

WHISK cream into melted chocolate. Mix in almond extract and Amaretto.

ADD 3/4 cup chopped praline. Pour into pie pan and freeze.

MIXTURE will be sticky/gooey. Scoop by teaspoon and shape into balls. Roll each ball in reserved chopped praline and then place in candy paper cups.

REFRIGERATE several hours before serving.

ALMOND PRALINE:

1 cup sugar

1/2 cup water

1 1/4 cups whole almonds

BOIL sugar and water together until syrup reaches soft ball stage or forms ball in cold water.

ADD whole almonds to syrup and boil to crack stage, or until it separates into threads in cold water. If liquid becomes grainy, add a few tablespoons of water, brushing down sides of pan to dissolve crystals. Continue to cook to crack stage.

POUR onto greased cookie sheet. Cool and chop to desired fineness.

NOTE: A candy thermometer works best for this recipe.

Mints for Frangophiles

The following recipe comes from Judy Frizzell of Sedro Woolley. Warning*: these chocolate mints can be addictive.*

MAKES 64 MINTS.

3/4 pound candy-making milk chocolate

1 package mint or regular semi-sweet chocolate chips

2 tablespoons melted shortening

1/4 cup scalded whipping cream, cooled to lukewarm

Peppermint extract to taste

MELT the two kinds of chocolate together in microwave or in top of double boiler. Pour into deep mixing bowl.

ADD melted shortening a little at a time, beating well between additions with electric mixer.

ADD scalded cream and peppermint all at once. Mix slowly until smooth, then beat on highest speed for one minute.

PLACE bowl in refrigerator until chocolate is lukewarm, about ten minutes. Don't let it get cold or hard.

BEAT again for two minutes on high and pour mixture into buttered 8x8-inch pan.

WHEN FIRM, cut into 1-inch squares. Sift unsweetened cocoa over mints and store in air-tight container.

Brown Cakes

A three-generation family favorite Swedish cookie from Skagit City's pioneer Tillie Larson, via daughter Alde Hastie and granddaughter Phyllis Keily-Tyler.

MAKES APPROXIMATELY 5 DOZEN COOKIES.

1 cup margarine

1 cup sugar

2 cups flour

1 teaspoon soda

2 teaspoons vanilla sugar (see note)

2 tablespoons Lyle's Golden Syrup*

*If you can't find Lyle's Golden Syrup, a British favorite, you can substitute corn syrup for a slightly different consistency and flavor.

PREHEAT oven to 350°.

CREAM margarine and sugar together in mixing bowl and add sifted dry ingredients.

STIR in syrup until mixture is smooth.

DIVIDE dough into 4 portions. Form each portion into 15-inch roll the diameter of a wiener.

SET rolls on ungreased cookie sheets, two to a sheet. Allow space between as rolls will flatten out as they bake.

BAKE for 15 minutes or until cookie dough is lightly browned.

CUT dough into 1-inch diagonal strips while warm and remove immediately from cookie sheet to towel to cool. (Alde uses a pastry wheel to cut her strips. If they cool on the cookie sheet they are very difficult to remove from the pan.)

NOTE: Make your own vanilla sugar by placing split vanilla beans in pint of sugar and store in closed container for one week to one month.

Sour Cherry Cream Cheese Cookies

Alde Larson Hastie's Sour Cherry Cream Cheese Cookies taste a lot like cherry pie. Delicious and easy to make.

MAKES APPROXIMATELY 6 DOZEN 2-INCH OR 4 1/2 DOZEN 2 1/2-INCH COOKIES.

1 cup butter

4 1/2 ounces low-fat cream cheese

2 cups flour

1 small jar sour cherry jam

Powdered sugar for dusting

PREHEAT oven to 375°.

MIX room-temperature butter and cream cheese in a mixing bowl and stir in flour.

ROLL dough out between pieces of plastic wrap into a rectangle about 1/4 inch thick.

USE 2-inch to 2 1/2-inch round cookie cutter to shape cookies.

MAKE each cookie into a cornucopia shape by overlapping 2 lower edges to form narrow part of cornucopia shape. Press the overlapped end firmly but gently with finger.

FILL open part with cherry jam and place on ungreased cookie sheet.

BAKE for 12 to 15 minutes or until lightly browned.

REMOVE from cookie sheet while warm. Cool and dust with powdered sugar.

Dorcelée's Melting Moments Cookies

Try these with Skagit Wild Blackberry Chantilly *(page 174).*

MAKES THREE DOZEN COOKIES.

1/2 cup corn starch
1/2 cup powdered sugar
1 cup all-purpose flour
3/4 cup margarine
1 teaspoon grated orange zest

PREHEAT oven to 300°.

SIFT dry ingredients together.

WORK IN margarine and orange zest to make soft dough.

CHILL dough for about one hour.

FORM dough into 1/2-inch balls and place on ungreased cookie sheet.

FLATTEN with floured fork.

BAKE for 20-25 minutes or until set.

Camille's Soda Cracker Cookies

Roz Spray of Bayview has her sister Camille to thank for this recipe. These cookies are simple to make and taste a lot like Tacoma's famous Almond Roca.

MAKES APPROXIMATELY 4 DOZEN COOKIES.

Soda crackers

1 cup sugar

1 cup butter

1 12-ounce package chocolate chips

1 cup sliced almonds

PREHEAT oven to 400°.

LINE 11x15-inch shallow pan or cookie sheet with foil.

LAY single layer of soda crackers on foil.

IN SAUCEPAN, cook sugar and butter over medium heat for 3 to 4 minutes, stirring constantly.

POUR mixture over crackers and bake for 5 minutes.

REMOVE from oven and sprinkle chocolate chips over entire surface of crackers. As they melt, spread evenly.

SPRINKLE almonds over chocolate, chill.

WHEN FIRM cut into 3-inch squares.

Sugar Cookies

Katherine Weckerly and her husband have enjoyed retirement for 26 years up on the Cascade River Road near Marblemount. They came to the area from Seattle to work for City Light in 1951 and stayed. The following recipe is a favorite of Katherine's granddaughters.

MAKES 4 1/2 TO 5 DOZEN 2-INCH COOKIES.

3/4 cup shortening or margarine

1 1/4 cups sugar

1 egg

1 teaspoon vanilla

1/2 teaspoon lemon flavoring (optional)

3 1/2 cups sifted flour

1 teaspoon baking soda

1/2 teaspoon salt

1/2 cup buttermilk

PREHEAT oven to 350°.

CREAM margarine, sugar, eggs, vanilla, and lemon flavoring (if used) with mixer on high speed until fluffy.

SIFT dry ingredients together and with mixer on low speed, add to creamed mixture alternately with buttermilk.

ADD more flour, if needed, to make a stiff dough. Chill.

ROLL OUT dough, cut in various shapes, and place on lightly greased cookie sheet.

BAKE for 12-15 minutes.

NOTE: This recipe can be used as the base for Fruit Pizza (page 181). Use 2/3 of dough for pizza and 1/3 for cookies as above.

Apple Pie—Aunt Pete's Prize Winner

A favorite from Bill Stendal, mayor of Sedro Woolley. In Bill's words, "This is truly an old family recipe. My 90-year-old Aunt Pete entered her apple pie in the Oregon State Fair and won a blue ribbon with this recipe."

MAKES 1 PIE.

1 quart Bill's canned apples *(recipe follows)*

1/2 cup sugar

4 tablespoons flour

1/2 teaspoon cinnamon

PREHEAT oven to 425°.

COMBINE all ingredients in mixing bowl, stirring lightly.

POUR into unbaked 9-inch pastry shell *(recipe follows)*.

DOT with butter.

ADD top crust, fluting edges, and cut decorative vents in center of pie crust.

BAKE for 30 minutes.

BILL'S PIE CRUST:

4 cups flour

2 teaspoons salt

1 3/4 cups yellow shortening

2 eggs, beaten

4 tablespoons white vinegar

Makes 4 9-inch pie crusts.

COMBINE flour and salt.

CUT IN shortening with pastry blender or two knives.

ADD eggs mixed with vinegar and stir with fork until dough forms cohesive ball.

DIVIDE dough into 4 balls. Roll each out to make 10-inch rounds.

NOTE: Dough can be frozen or recipe halved.

BILL'S CANNED APPLES FOR APPLE PIE:

PEEL, core, and slice 6 gallons of Gravenstein apples (1 30-pound box).

PLACE them in stone crock or plastic container, 1 gallon at a time.

AS EACH GALLON of apple slices is added, sprinkle 1 cup sugar over them. Do not stir. Cover container with damp cloth.

Makes 19 quarts.

LET APPLE SLICES STAND for 24 hours.

STIR apple slices, drain (reserve juice), and pack in sterilized jars.

POUR reserved juice over apple slices, adding equal amounts to each jar. Do not add any other liquid.

SEAL and process jars 20 minutes in boiling water bath.

Norwegian Apple Pie

This recipe is a favorite from the late State Senator Lowell Peterson's kitchen. He represented the Upper Skagit Valley for many years.

MAKES 2 8-INCH PIES.

1 1/2 cups sugar

1 cup flour

2 teaspoons baking powder

1 teaspoon salt

1/2 teaspoon cinnamon

1/2 teaspoon nutmeg

2 eggs

1 tablespoon vanilla

2 to 3 cups apples, diced

1/2 cup walnuts, chopped

PREHEAT oven to 350°.

SIFT all dry ingredients together in mixing bowl.

ADD eggs, vanilla, diced apples, and walnuts.

GREASE two 8-inch pie pans and divide mixture between them.

BAKE for 35 to 40 minutes. Pie makes its own crust.

SERVE warm with your favorite whipped topping.

Shaker Lemon Pie

This pie is for the lemon lovers of the world. The secret to its success is paper-thin slices. If you are lucky enough to own a mandoline slicer, now's the time to use it. Otherwise, sharpen your knife!

MAKES 1 9-INCH PIE.

2 large lemons

2 cups sugar

4 eggs, well beaten

Double pie crust

PREHEAT oven to 450°.

CUT OFF lemon ends and discard.

SLICE lemons as thin as paper, rind and all.

COMBINE lemon slices with sugar. Mix well and let stand 2 hours or longer, stirring occasionally.

ADD beaten eggs to lemon mixture and mix well.

TURN mixture into 9-inch unbaked pie shell and arrange lemon slices evenly.

COVER with top crust. Cut several slits near center.

BAKE for 15 minutes.

REDUCE HEAT to 375° and bake for about 20 minutes or until silver knife inserted near edge of pie comes out clean.

COOL pie before serving or serve it slightly warm. Serve small portions; flavor is highly concentrated.

Lemon-Lime Pie

An old Date Book for 1911 that contained this recipe has lain around my house for many years. It is filled with spidery handwritten recipes for everything from fig wine and Tillings Bitters to sourdough starter and desserts that melt in your mouth. This is my favorite.

MAKES 1 9-INCH PIE.

3 egg yolks
2 tablespoons flour
1/2 cup sugar
1/3 cup fresh lime juice
1/3 cup fresh lemon juice
1/2 teaspoon lime peel, grated
1/2 teaspoon lemon peel, grated
1/3 cup boiling water

PREHEAT oven to 325°.

IN THE TOP of a double boiler, off heat, beat egg yolks until thick and lemony.

SIFT together flour and sugar and beat into yolks.

ADD juices and grated peels and continue to beat until well mixed.

GRADUALLY BEAT in boiling water.

TRANSFER top of double boiler (with contents) to stove. Set into base of double boiler containing boiling water. Whisk contents continually until custard is thick.

MERINGUE:
3 egg whites
3 tablespoons sugar

IN A SEPARATE BOWL, beat egg whites until peaks start to form. While beating, gradually add 3 tablespoons sugar.

WHEN MIXTURE HOLDS its shape, fold gently into custard.

COOL slightly and pour into prebaked 9-inch pie shell.

BROWN delicately in preheated oven, about 10 minutes. Cool and serve.

Fresh Raspberry Pie

Therese Ovenell was born in the Skagit Valley and has lived here all her life. She shared several recipes with me that show off the Valley's fruit and meat products in a speedy yet delicious way. I have served the following fresh raspberry pie repeatedly this berry season and it receives high marks every time. You can make the pastry shell from Jetska Koop's Dutch Piecrust recipe (see page 199). Or, if you are really in a hurry, use a frozen deep dish pie crust from the freezer section of your favorite market.

MAKES 1 9-INCH PIE.

1 9-Inch baked and cooled pie shell

4 cups fresh raspberries

GLAZE:

1 cup sugar

2 tablespoons cornstarch

1 1/2 cups water

1 3-ounce package raspberry Jello

IN MEDIUM SAUCEPAN, stir together sugar and cornstarch.

ADD water and whisk mixture with wire whip.

COOK over medium heat until thick and clear. Stir jello into hot mixture until well blended and pour over berries in pie shell.

REFRIGERATE until set.

SERVE pie with whipped cream or Kool Whip. Reserve some fresh raspberries to garnish with dollop of whipped cream on each serving.

NOTE: Fresh strawberries and strawberry jello are another great combination.

Winter Pear Delight

I can't tell you how delicious this pie is; you just have to try it.

MAKES 1 9-INCH PIE.

4 to 5 large winter pears (preferably Comice), peeled and sliced

3 tablespoons frozen orange juice concentrate

1/2 teaspoon lemon zest

PREHEAT oven to 350°.

TOSS pears, juice, and zest together in mixing bowl and pour into unbaked 9-inch pie crust.

SPRINKLE topping *(see below)* over pie and bake until fruit is tender and topping is nicely browned, 35 to 50 minutes.

TOPPING:

3/4 cup flour

1/2 cup brown sugar

1/2 teaspoon ginger

1/2 teaspoon cinnamon

6 tablespoons melted butter

1/2 cup walnuts, chopped

IN A MIXING BOWL, combine all ingredients with fork.

NOTE: Serve pie warm with whipped cream sweetened with 2 tablespoons of Grand Marnier instead of sugar. Decadent! Or try a small scoop of Swiss almond ice cream.

Dutch Pie Crust

Jetska Koops came from Holland to the Skagit Valley in the early part of this century to become the bride of another Hollander in America, Jake Koops Sr. For many years the Koops family maintained a grocery store in Lyman that carried everything from calked logging boots to fresh meat and produce. During the 1950s, as soon as the school bus left with my children, Jetska beckoned me over for our coffee hour. She told me many stories of the trials of her early days in the Valley as we sat and drank her strong European coffee accompanied by Dutch rusks that she buttered and sprinkled with tiny, anise-flavored candies. We shared many recipes. This is one of hers I have used for 40 years.

MAKES 4 SHELLS OR 2 DOUBLE PIE CRUSTS.

2 cups shortening

4 cups flour

1 teaspoon baking powder

1 teaspoon sugar

1 teaspoon salt

1 egg

1 tablespoon white vinegar

Cold water

PREHEAT oven to 425°.

CUT shortening into dry ingredients.

BEAT egg in measuring cup with fork, add vinegar, and pour in enough cold water to make 3/4 cup.

STIR liquid mixture into flour-shortening mixture until it forms a solid mass.

ROLL OUT dough on lightly floured pastry cloth or board.

BAKE shells 10 minutes or until lightly browned. For double crusts follow individual recipe baking directions.

NOTE: This pie crust freezes well or recipe can be halved.

Easy Trifle

From Maureen Johnson of Big Lake, a dessert that looks as elegant as it tastes. Serve this trifle in a crystal bowl or in parfait glasses.

SERVES 10.

2 packages frozen raspberries

4 teaspoons cornstarch

1 can condensed milk

1 cup cold water

1 small package instant vanilla pudding mix

2 cups whipping cream

1 small pound cake, Sara Lee frozen*

1/4 cup orange juice

1/3 cup almonds, sliced

*Or use sponge cake, preferably day-old, or any plain leftover cake.

DRAIN raspberries and save 1 cup of their juice. Combine saved juice with cornstarch and cook until clear and thickened. Chill.

MIX condensed milk with water and stir into pudding mix. Beat until well blended. Chill 5 minutes.

WHIP cream and fold into chilled pudding.

CUT cake into bite-sized cubes. Place layer of cake cubes in large bowl. Sprinkle with orange juice. Add layer of raspberries, 1/2 juice syrup, 1/2 pudding and then repeat all layers. (Create similar layers if using individual parfait glasses.)

CHILL at least one hour before serving. Sprinkle nuts over top.

NOTE: The English gave trifle its name because the ingredients can be a trifle of this and a trifle of that. It often was a hurry-up dessert for unexpected company. Trifle takes on a more festive flavor if you substitute any orange liquer for the orange juice.

Steamed Christmas Pudding

This traditional English Christmas pudding has been served in Ruth Trueman Crawford's family for over a century. The Truemans arrived in Skagit county before 1900 from the Bollington area of England and settled in Lyman.

SERVES 10.

2 1/2 cups flour

1/4 teaspoon salt

1/4 teaspoon cloves

1/4 teaspoon nutmeg

1 teaspoon soda

1 teaspoon cinnamon

1 cup sour milk*

1 cup molasses

1 cup suet, finely chopped

1/2 to 1 cup raisins

*Can make sour milk by adding lemon juice to sweet milk until tastes sour.

WASH raisins and set aside.

SIFT dry ingredients together into mixing bowl.

COMBINE molasses and milk and add to dry ingredients.

STIR in suet and raisins.

FILL greased empty 1-pound coffee cans 3/4 full with batter and cover with foil. Place in top of steamer rack in tall kettle over several inches of water.

STEAM for 3 hours. Watch to make sure kettle doesn't boil dry; refill as needed.

RUN palette knife round edge of can to ensure pudding is not sticking and turn out pudding carefully.

POUR caramel sauce *(below)* over pudding. Add final dollop of Hard Sauce for rich finish.

CARAMEL SAUCE:

1 cup sugar

1/2 tablespoon cornstarch

1 cup cold water

IN HEAVY PAN or skillet, brown sugar (stirring constantly so it doesn't burn) until caramelized. Dissolve cornstarch in water. Stir into sugar and cook until thickened. Add more water to thin to desired consistency.

HARD SAUCE:

1/2 cup sweet butter

2 cups powdered sugar

1 teaspoon vanilla extract

BLEND together until smooth and place small dollop on top of sauced pudding. Vary the hard sauce flavor by adding small amount of lemon juice and grated lemon rind, or orange juice and rind, brandy, or cream sherry.

Burnt Cream Custard

Burnt Cream is a popular dessert at Tore Dybfest's two restaurants, the Farmhouse Inn at Highway 20 and LaConner-Whitney-Road and The Lighthouse Inn in LaConner.

SERVES 6.

2 cups cream

4 egg yolks

1/2 cup sugar

1 tablespoon vanilla extract

PREHEAT oven to 350°.

HEAT cream over low heat until bubbles form around edge of pan.

BEAT egg yolks and sugar together until thick, about 3 minutes.

GRADUALLY BEAT cream into yolks.

STIR in vanilla and pour into six 6-ounce custard cups.

PLACE custard cups in flat baking pan with 1/2 inch water in bottom.

BAKE for 45 minutes or until custard is set.

COOL, then chill, covered, in refrigerator for 1 hour.

SPRINKLE each custard with 2 teaspoons sugar. Place on top rack under broiler until medium brown. Chill before serving.

Cranberry Gifta

Laurie Olds of Fir Island contributed this century-old Norwegian traditional holiday recipe. She always has this one on her Christmas table.

SERVES 8.

4 cups cranberries

2 cups water

2 cups sugar

1 1/2 cups saltine cracker crumbs

1/8 cup butter, melted

1 1/2 cups cream, whipped

1/4 cup powdered sugar

1/2 teaspoon vanilla extract

BOIL cranberries in water until outer skins split.

ADD sugar and stir until dissolved. Return mixture to boiling.

REMOVE from heat. Cover.

COOL to room temperature.

IN SEPARATE BOWL, combine crumbs and butter.

FOLD powdered sugar and vanilla into whipped cream.

LAYER ingredients in clear glass bowl. Line with 1/3 cracker crumb mixture, then 1/3 cranberry mixture, then whipped cream.

REPEAT 3 layers. Sprinkle with a few plain cracker crumbs.

Marsala Wine Sherbet

A superb dessert served with berries or peaches, or alone with biscotti on the side, from Anne McCracken. She suggests experimenting with different wines like Madeira or any good sherry.

SERVES 6.

2 eggs

1/2 cup sugar

1/2 cup light corn syrup

1/2 cup half-and-half

1 teaspoon or more fresh lemon zest

6 tablespoons Marsala

4 tablespoons fresh lemon juice

BEAT eggs until lemon colored.

ADD sugar and beat until thick.

STIR in corn syrup, half-and-half, lemon zest, Marsala and lemon juice.

FREEZE mixture until almost firm.

BEAT until smooth, return to freezer and freeze until firm.

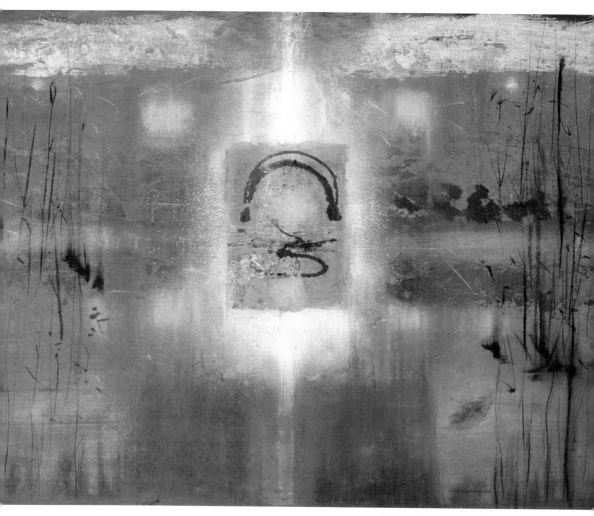

Equinox, Anne Martin McCool

BEVERAGES

THE TOAST

May you always have art to charm
your days, a sensible hearth
and friends as dependable as gravity.
May the wind and creatures be as music
to your evenings alone and may your dreams
leave you renewed. May you have an appaloosa
to ride the outline of blue hills, and nothing
that sickens, and no black sticks.

—JAMES BERTOLINO

Hot Spiced Apple Cider

Every year our old orchard of heirloom apples produces many gallons of apple cider. I can some in half-gallon jars and freeze the rest. This is a drink for all ages.

MAKES 16 1-CUP SERVINGS.

1 gallon fresh or thawed frozen apple cider

2 cinnamon sticks, broken into several pieces

12 whole cloves

1 orange, unpeeled and sliced thin

ADD spices and sliced orange to apple cider in a large saucepan.

HEAT slowly over low heat; do not boil.

SERVE in heat-proof cups.

Raspberry Punch

Especially refreshing in summer, this all-occasion punch can be served year around.

MAKES 20 1/2-CUP SERVINGS.

1 package frozen raspberries, mashed

6 cans raspberry pop

2 12-ounce cans frozen orange juice concentrate

1 quart cranberry juice

1 quart apple juice

STIR all ingredients together and pour into punch bowl.

Arts Commission Punch

Pauline Hunter Heath, a third-generation Skagitonian, shares her favorite non-alcoholic punch.

MAKES APPROXIMATELY 50 1/2-CUP SERVINGS.

4 ripe bananas

1 12-ounce can frozen orange juice, un-diluted

1 12-ounce can frozen limeade, undi-luted

1 12-ounce can frozen lemonade, undi-luted

1/2 bag ice cubes

1 46-ounce can apricot nectar

1 46-ounce can pineapple juice

2 2-liter bottles 7-UP or lemon-lime soda

Strawberry or kiwi slices, for garnish

BLEND first 4 ingredients in two batches and combine in mixing bowl.

POUR mixture into a ring mold (or other mold that will fit into punch bowl) and freeze.

JUST BEFORE SERVING, put ice cubes in punch bowl. Remove frozen block from mold and push down into ice cubes in punch bowl.

POUR apricot nectar, pineapple juice, and 7-UP over top.

GARNISH with strawberry or kiwi slices.

NOTE: Add one more liter of 7-UP to extend if needed.

Swedish Hot Punch

The ingredients for this authentic Julglogg can all be combined (except for vodka) ahead of time and stored, tightly covered, in the refrigerator.

MAKES 12 TO 14 1-CUP SERVINGS.

1 750ml-bottle claret wine*
1 750ml-bottle ruby port
1 fifth vodka
12 cardamon seeds
6 whole cloves
1 cinnamon stick
Peel from 1 orange, slivered
1 cup blanched almonds
1 cup raisins
3/4 cup sugar

*Burgundy may be substituted.

COMBINE all ingredients except vodka in stainless steel or enameled pan and heat to just boiling.

JUST BEFORE SERVING, add vodka and heat again to boiling.

IF YOU ARE BRAVE, follow Swedish tradition and set punch aflame for a few seconds.

SERVE punch immediately in mugs with handles. Supply small spoons to scoop up raisins and almonds.

KEEP PUNCH HOT on electric warming tray or over burner of chafing dish.

Corky's Glug

A great drink for a cold winter night.

MAKES 12 1-CUP SERVINGS.

2 quarts apple cider
1 6-ounce can undiluted frozen lemonade
2 cups wine (rose or chablis)
2 cinnamon sticks
1 or 2 oranges studded with whole
   cloves
Ground nutmeg to taste

MIX all ingredients well in large pot.

HEAT over low heat until hot but do not boil.

SERVE in mugs or glass cups.

May Wine

This festive spring-into-summer drink is a specialty of mine for parties. I especially like to make it when the sweet woodruff near my kitchen door is blooming. The tiny white flowers floating next to the bright berries in the punch bowl make a striking combination.

MAKES APPROXIMATELY 24 1/2-CUP SERVINGS.

3 liters of Rhine wine

1/2 cup sweet woodruff, new growth only

1 orange, sliced

1 lemon, sliced

1 cup strawberries, sliced or whole raspberries

COMBINE all ingredients in large covered glass container and refrigerate for one hour before pouring into punch bowl.

Wild Rose Petal Wine

I have a pleasant memory of floating down the Skagit in my canoe and visiting artist Michael Clough's home on an Island in the middle of the river. Michael served this nectar-like wine made from wild rose petals.

MAKES 1 GALLON.

1 gallon water
1 gallon (16 cups) loosely packed wild
    rose petals.
2 pounds sugar
1 handful of raisens
1 packet wine yeast

BOIL water and pour over petals in bucket or crock and let stand for 24 hours.

SQUEEZE juice from petals back into container and discard petals.

HEAT half of the juice with 2 pounds of sugar. Add handful of chopped raisins and continue to heat until sugar is dissolved.

PUT BACK into container, cool to lukewarm temperature (about 100°), and add 1 packet wine yeast.

COVER container and stir daily.

AFTER ABOUT 10 DAYS, when yeast frothing subsides, strain into gallon jug.

TOP OFF with as much water as needed to fill jug and put airlock on jug.

RACK after 1 month and top jug again with water. (Racking is the process of siphoning off the clear wine into another jug, leaving behind any sediment or impurities, such as petal debris or yeast particles, that might impair the flavor and color.)

START DRINKING during the next rose-petal season.

Susan's Frozen Rum Daiquiri

A pair of special drinks from a local cookbook. The first is a great summer cooler that can be frozen weeks ahead and will refreeze IF any is left over.

SERVES 8 TO 10.

1 fifth white rum
1 12 1/2-ounce can frozen limeade
1 liter bottle 7-UP or Sprite
3/4 cup water
Lime slices for garnish

COMBINE all ingredients in large container.

FREEZE in two 1-quart airtight containers.

REMOVE containers as needed from freezer. Thaw just to the stage where mixture can be stirred until smooth and mushy.

POUR in appropriate glasses and garnish with lime.

Hawaiian Chi Chi

SERVES 2.

2 ounces vodka
4 ounces pineapple juice
2 ounces coconut syrup
1 ounce lemon juice
Handful of ice cubes

COMBINE all liquids in blender.

ADD ice cubes and blend until smooth.

POUR into glasses and serve.

NOTE: For pina colada, substitute rum for vodka.

OLD SKAGIT VALLEY BARNS

Old valley barns
sag
like ancient
Chinese coolies.
Sway.
Blur like cataracted eyes.
They slip into earth.
Nobody hears them
fall.

—GLEN TURNER

Afterword

I HAVE LIVED IN AND LOVED THE SKAGIT VALLEY for more than fifty years. The Upper Valley—earth of my childhood, sometimes struggling, often joyous—created a solid foundation for my life. I will always remember that mountainous, backwoods womb and growing up on a forty-acre stump ranch, high on a hillside of the South Skagit between Concrete and Rockport, accessible only by a hand-wound ferry. The Faber Ferry opened for travel at six a.m. and closed down at midnight. The operater lived in a cabin across the river from our home. If you had an emergency during his off-duty hours, you had to pound on a loud gong or honk your horn for long periods.

Home, then, was a hand-hewn cedar shake house, inside and out. Windows facing across the valley, dominated by the craggy vista of Sauk Mountain. So many memories. Lullaby sleep to the soughing breeze, fingering, combing great fir branches. The woman's scream of cougar, leaping from fir tree, to roof, to ground. Each primal scream goose-bumping my being. Twilight, and the bear growling over the compost heap. I remember dropping the pail of potato peelings and hitting the kitchen door at a hard run; father claimed it was still swinging a week later. The Saturday nights my father laid aside all work and filled our little house with Irish music. I danced to his harmonica from the day I learned to walk until the day I left home at seventeen.

Daily rituals of cleaning the chimneys of the kerosene Aladdin lamps, carrying all our water up a steep hill from a fast-running, cold creek. The flat irons heated on the old Monarch wood stove (my mother was a stickler about ironing every stitch of clothes). Helping prepare meals, baby-sitting younger siblings, doing endless dishes. During the summer, canning all the excess garden vegetables. We also canned venison, chicken, grouse, beef — you name it. Once a week was baking day, at least ten loaves per baking. Between chores, secreting myself with a favorite book under the tallest ferns. Lost in make-believe adventures, emerging only when the tone of my name being called took on a certain timbre.

Our seasons were marked by Sauk Mountain's changing robes. Spring snow melting down its face, gradually turning the meadows into every nuance of green, tender to verdant; summer often announced by great cloud banks with sudden thunderstorms unleashing a frenetic fury, lightning dancing across Sauk's craggy knobs, torching tall twisted trees on the mountainside. Late summer brought a haze of wildflowers; fireweed, Indian paintbrush, lupine, heather; early fall, a riot of vine maple color. In late fall, dustings of snow appeared on its rocky crown; winter draped a heavy mantle. To this day, Sauk Mountain is a special place for me. I first climbed it at age fourteen. My first-ever big mountain hike. At that time, it was a 10-mile hike that started on a forest service trail beyond Rockport. The forest fire lookout is gone from its highest point, but the mountain is much the same. This year, 1994, it abounded with wildflowers, pikas, and whistling marmots when I was at its summit in August—as it did on that first climb, nearly fifty years ago.

In 1949, three days after high school graduation, I began my life's journey down the Skagit. A child bride, becoming farm-schooled, birthing three children by age twenty-one. Growing up with those children and loving it. Always on the land, growing things, cooking, canning. While living at Lyman I could still see Sauk Mountain when I looked upriver. During this period of my life in the valley I learned to appreciate the richness and diversity of our valley's cultural heritage. The Skagit Valley has more than just physical beauty. The multitude of settler groups has left a heritage of traditions and work ethics to be retained and cherished.

In 1972, I traveled down the last segment of the Skagit River Valley to Fir Island, cradled between the forks of the Skagit. Here I have found a haven of fertile loam. My life's love of the land expands as the gardens I tend expand: sunflowers fifteen feet tall, vegetables and fruit glowing, growing. The bird life so diverse, so beautiful. My seasonal calendar is now attuned to their migrations. Another month from this writing, the first of the trumpeter swans will announce their arrival at dusk. Who wouldn't love this valley?

—LAVONE NEWELL

LIST OF PAINTINGS

On the Cover
Currier, Alfred
Skagit Tulips
Oil, 44" x 50"

Page 17
Graves, Morris
Winter Still Life (hellebore)
Watercolor and tempera on paper
26" x 44"
Collection of the artist

Page 67
Gilkey, Richard
River Landscape
Oil, 31" x 42"

Page 109
Wilder, Maggie
The Teacher
Oil on canvas, 45" x 51"

Page 127
James, Clayton
Winter Fields, Fir Island
Oil, 16" x 20"

Page 145
McCracken, Philip
Exploding Potato
Mixed media on paper,
25-3/8" x 30-3/8"

Page 171
Anderson, Guy
Triumph of the Egg
Oil on paper, 96" x 48"
Collection of T. R. Welch

Page 205
McCool, Anne Martin
Equinox
Acrylic on canvas, 36" x 50"

LIST OF POEMS

Page 18
Sunflower, *The Sacred Round—Poems from an Island Garden,* Thelma Palmer, Island Publishers, Anacortes, WA, 1985.

Page 33
Last Sunset Of The Year 1975: Fishtown, and Lines On Being Poor, *Rimes of a River Rat,* Paul Hansen, printed by Paul Hansen, LaConner, WA, 1978.

Page 50
Gardens, *The Sacred Round—Poems from an Island Garden,* Thelma Palmer, Island Publishers, Anacortes, WA, 1985.

Page 68
Heron, *Heron Light,* Clifford Burke, Brooding Heron Press, Waldron Island, WA, 1968.

Page 92
Rookery, Rock Sound, *Eleven Skagit Poets,* Bill Slater, Brooding Heron Press, Waldron Island, WA, 1987.

Page 110
Squash, James Bertolino, *First Credo, Quarterly Review of Literature Poetry Series,* Princeton Univ., Princeton, NJ, 1986.

Page 128
Two Roads On The Same Day (Broadside), Peter Heffelfinger, The Co-op Press, Anacortes, WA.

Page 146
God Grant the Practical Shape Our Days, *Eleven Skagit Poets,* Jean Haight, Brooding Heron Press, Waldron Island, WA, 1987.

Page 172
House, *Ish River,* Robert Sund, North Point Press, San Francisco, CA, 1983.

Page 206
The Toast, James Bertolino, *First Credo, Quarterly Review of Literature Poetry Series,* Princeton Univ., Princeton, NJ, 1986

Page 214
Old Skagit Valley Barns, *Redding Leaves,* Glen Turner, Tamarack Press, LaConner, WA, 1979.

Index